W9-DHV-592

Ron Bowman

Other books by Diane Kennedy Pike

THE OTHER SIDE (*with James A. Pike*)
SEARCH
THE WILDERNESS REVOLT (*with R. Scott Kennedy*)
CHANNELING LOVE ENERGY (*with Arleen Lorrance*)

DIANE KENNEDY PIKE

LIFE IS

VICTORIOUS!

HOW TO GROW THROUGH GRIEF
A Personal Experience

SIMON AND SCHUSTER
NEW YORK

Copyright © 1976 by Diane Kennedy Pike
All rights reserved
including the right of reproduction
in whole or in part in any form
Published by Simon and Schuster
A Gulf+Western Company
Rockefeller Center, 630 Fifth Avenue
New York, New York 10020

Designed by Elizabeth Woll
Manufactured in the United States of America

1   2   3   4   5   6   7   8   9   10

Library of Congress Cataloging in Publication Data

Pike, Diane Kennedy.
Life is victorious!

1. Pike, Diane Kennedy. 2. Pike, James Albert,
Bp., 1913-1969. 3. Grief. I. Title.
BR1725.P54A34   242'.4   76-17328
ISBN 0-671-22335-6

ACKNOWLEDGMENTS

MY THANKS go to all those who stood beside me during my grief, accepting me exactly as I was, offering comfort when I sought it, and in no way interfering with my grief process.

First and foremost is my brother, R. Scott Kennedy, who came to be with me during the search for my husband in the desert, who dropped out of school for a quarter to live and travel with me so that I wouldn't be alone, and who was a best friend to me while I was grieving.

I am also most grateful to my parents, Arlene and Ed Kennedy, who were loving and wise parents to me as I grieved, as they have been during my whole life.

I am grateful to Jim, who shared himself fully with me and did not remove himself from me even in death.

And to so many other family members and friends who gave themselves to me in love: Ellen and John Downing, Gertrude Platt, Pearl Chambers, Patricia Bradley, to mention a few.

I am also grateful to Jean Askew, Mary Louise Shoolery, and Betsey Somerville for their unique gifts of self which sparked me to new depths of growth and understanding, and to Laurel Keyes and Hannah Hurnard for being open channels through which I touched new heights and depths of my Higher Self.

My thanks, again, to Scott Kennedy and Arleen Lorrance and Tamara Comstock for reading the manuscript in its infant stages and offering their helpful comments and suggestions, and to Gertrude Platt for her help in typing the manuscript.

I also offer thanks for the thoughts and prayers of so many who wished me well during that entire time of growth and whose Love/Life Energy strengthened my own, as well as for those who challenged and prodded me from their very different-from-mine frames of reference and points of view.

Most of all, I am grateful for my own willingness to go fully into grief and experience its depths, for the Life Force that moves in me and makes such an experience possible, and for the power to be conscious with which I Am.

DIANE K. PIKE

To
my brother and close friend
R. Scott Kennedy
for being who he is
for sharing my life
for doing his own lifework

CONTENTS

PREFACE

GRIEF IS OUR RESPONSE to physical separation, usually by death, from one with whom we have been in a close, loving relationship. Grief is a part of the natural-order process of growth in the realm of personal relationships. Most persons who have grieved find they have a great deal in common, not only because they have suffered but also because the phases and patterns of their pain are very much alike.

In a book called *Up from Grief: Patterns of Recovery,** the authors point out that hundreds of interviews with widows, widowers, and parents who have lost children revealed that, although there were great variations in the amount of time spent in each facet of the process and in the details of the experiencing, yet almost without exception persons in grief began with a period of *shock*, then entered a time of *suffering*, and finally went through a period of building a new life for themselves, or *recovery*.

I read Kreis and Pattie's book while I was grieving and

* By Bernadine Kreis and Alice Pattie, New York: The Seabury Press, 1969.

13

found it a great comfort to know that others had been through much that I was then experiencing. Although I am aware that the details of how death came into my life and of how I faced my grief vary from the experiences of others, I feel confident there will be much in my story with which anyone will readily identify. Therefore, I share my whole experience, hoping that it will be of some comfort to those who are in the midst of the grief process.

I also share in detail for and with those who are friends or relatives of persons who are grieving and who might like to understand more of the process their loved one is going through. I offer my story as a window through which to view the inner experience of one who grieves.

My principal intent is to offer a broader perspective on grief, not just for those who have had, or are having, the experience, but perhaps just as much for those who have not yet entered it. Perhaps my story will open up new possibilities for those who seek to live their lives in higher states of consciousness.

By relating how I responded to grief as an opportunity for growth in self-awareness and as an opportunity to experience life more deeply, I put forth one example for the reader's consideration of how to live in a state of higher consciousness while in the midst of times of so-called trouble. Often it seems easier to live in the joy and serenity of expanded awareness when all is going well in life, as we perceive it. But if we are to move into a new consciousness that, by its nature, comprehends the wholeness of life in the cosmic sense and transcends the viewpoint of isolated individualism, *and* if we are still to live in the body, manifesting as persons, we must learn to function fully in all kinds of life-experiences. I hope this book will be a contribution in that direction. I functioned with full awareness while deeply and totally experiencing the pain and trauma of grief, and found in the process as great an opportunity for growth as I have ever encountered.

14

The Facets of Self Held in Perspective

I grew enormously through grief. I learned a great deal about life and death, about suffering and compassion. I grew in my ability to receive love from others. I grew in self-confidence. I grew in self-knowledge. I discovered that to suffer a great deal of pain is to be greatly alive. I grew in my capacity to love.

You will find as you read my story that I refer to various "parts," or aspects, of myself: my body and my Little Self, my mind and my Higher Self. I began, after my breakthrough to cosmic consciousness and long before I entered grief, to view myself as expressing or manifesting through these four facets of being. I found growing through the grief, and sustaining my Higher Self awareness through it, far easier when I kept these four aspects of the whole "me" in perspective.

My body, of course, is my biological organism—the physical manifestation of my larger, or Higher, Self— which mirrors my state of consciousness, making it (me) visible and tangible. My physiological organism has its own life, in a sense, for it conforms to a set of laws inherent in the physical world. Consequently, those processes set in motion in the body must be completed in the body. I learned how fully this is so, in and through my grieving.

My Little Self is the feeling aspect of Self, or my emotional nature. It is the child within me, that potential to be the totally spontaneous, pure child of God, the child who, according to Jesus, will enable me to enter the Kingdom. My Little Self is also that aspect of me which very often falls into, or seems locked into, patterns of reacting and responding which I learned when I was physically a child.

My mind is that logical, computer-like memory bank that stores up all the data of my life experience and calls forth what is needed to analyze things, solve problems, or "think things through." It has no feelings at all, but it does carefully

15

take note of and record my feelings and the feelings of others in order to "make sense" out of them.

Higher Self is the intuitive, or "higher mind," aspect of me—my direct connection with the universal mind or intelligence, that is, with God. It is my lifeline to the overall plan for my life, to the perfect pattern for my life in this incarnation. It is God within me, the holy spirit filling my being. It was by functioning in and through my Higher Self that I was able to perceive grief as an opportunity for growth and to love myself through the entire grief process.*

Much of my growth came because of my awareness of these facets of my being, and grieving gave me many new insights into how I function in and through each of them. These insights have been helpful, in turn, in continuing to grow in my ability to live out of the awareness of higher consciousness while being fully in, and interacting with, the world as I experience it each day. I offer these insights in the hope they will help clarify the reader's own experiences, not only with regard to grief but in all situations that are trying or difficult.

I wish you growth through grief, through other times of trouble and trauma, and into the freedom, joy, and oneness of higher-consciousness living.

* For a full explication of this approach to viewing the self, see Diane K. Pike and Arleen Lorrance, *Channeling Love Energy*, LP Publications, P.O. Box 7601, San Diego, Ca. 92107; 1976.

LIFE IS
VICTORIOUS!

1

THE INGREDIENTS FOR GRIEF
Life Fully Shared with Another

I WAS TWENTY-EIGHT when I met Jim. At the time, I was in the process of deciding (again) whether "never" to marry or whether to marry the man I was dating.

I suppose most women who pass twenty-five without marrying begin to ask themselves if there is something wrong with them. I knew I liked men well enough, but somehow I could never bring myself to consider marriage seriously. Some element of sharing and commonality was always missing in the romantic relationships I established. I kept feeling that it was possible to find someone with whom I could *totally* share my being and life, and that if I didn't find such a person, to marry would be a compromise of my own being.

As the years went by, however, I began to question my own concept of a total relationship. Perhaps, as my father had often suggested, I was too idealistic. After all, I did not know many, if any, married couples who had such a completely whole union of sharing. Perhaps I should marry in the hope that the fullness would emerge in time.

My lawyer friend, whom I had dated rather seriously for some six months while I was living in New York City and had visited and written to since, was coming to California to spend the month of August. Both of us saw his visit as a time "to see." Perhaps we would marry. We were compatible enough in almost every way, and that "something" I felt to be missing was so intangible as to be almost inexpressible by words.

I was, at the time, working on the staff of a large United Methodist Church in Palo Alto, California, as director of Youth and Children's Work. My life had been centered in the Church since I was a little child. I had often fantasized meeting a minister with whom I could share my life, but in reality, I seldom met a minister who appealed to me as a man. "Secular" men, however—men whose lives and interests were focused on vocations and causes basically unrelated to the Church—were often exciting, interesting, and sexually appealing.

My lawyer friend, for instance, shared most of my values, but Church had been only a childhood thing for him. Now he was involved in causes, such as the civil rights movement, and felt the Church to be something of an "enemy," to be watched with suspicion. It was in this that the intangible "something" lay for me. I did not consider myself "pious," but I was deeply religious and totally committed to serving God in and through the Church. It seemed important to me to share that commitment with the man I would marry.

One Last Try

It occurred to me in that summer of 1966 to give that "something" one last try. I thought of taking some summer school classes at Pacific School of Religion in Berkeley. The classes would enrich me as a person and serve as further "training" for my work, and *perhaps* I would meet there a man, a minister, who would be "the" one. At least it was worth a try, and it was important to me to open myself once more to the possibility that I had not been waiting in vain. When Brad came in August, I would then have a clearer sense of what I did and did not want.

When the bulletin of summer school course offerings came, there were two that caught my eye at once. They were being offered on the same days—Tuesdays and Thursdays, morning and afternoon—and would thus simplify my commuting. Moreover, they were in subjects that fitted right in with my own stage of growth. The courses were entitled "The New Theology" and "The New Morality."

I had had a series of experiences about six months before which had totally altered my world view. I had broken through to cosmic consciousness. Since then, I had been rethinking all my values, attitudes, and beliefs. Surely these courses would be helpful to me in that process.

The classes were to be taught by James A. Pike, Bishop of the Episcopal Diocese of California, who, the bulletin reported, had just returned from a six-month sabbatical leave in England, where he had studied with many of the principal theologians of the movement known as the "New Theology." He was a spokesman in his own Church for the "growing edge" of both theology and ethics, the bulletin reported, and thus was eminently qualified to teach the two courses.

I was vaguely aware of Bishop Pike. I had seen his name in the newspapers, and though I had not really "followed" him in the news, I knew that he was a very controversial figure. I also remembered reading not long before of his son's death by suicide, and I recalled feeling great sympathy that such a personal tragedy had been made so public. More than that I did not recall, but it was enough. I would sign up for the classes.

My friend Pat Rohrs went with me on the day I enrolled. She knew my "real" motivation for taking the classes, so while I was filling out papers, she checked out the men who filed in and out, looking for "likely prospects," and then checked to see if they already wore wedding rings. Both she and I were a little disheartened, as it seemed nearly all the men were "too old" or already married, but I hoped there were others we had not seen. All I needed was "just one."

21

Student Meets Professor

The rest of the story sounds like something out of a book. On the first day of classes, I scanned the "audience" of my fellow students, looking for someone who would appeal to me. My interest was divided between my search for "a man" and the dynamic and fascinating person who was our teacher.

I found Bishop Pike surprisingly human, warm, articulate, and knowledgeable. He was a fascinating lecturer, had a wonderful sense of humor, and was a fine teacher. His mind was quick and challenging. Somehow I had not anticipated all these qualities in such a famous man. My previous experience had been that men who were at the top in their own fields did not relate very well to those "at the bottom." But Bishop Pike was different. I was enjoying his classes.

At the beginning of the afternoon break, Bishop Pike said, "Is anyone here going to San Francisco at the end of the class?" I had to drive that way on my way back to Palo Alto, so I raised my hand. He said, "Fine. I'll ride with you. I need a lift back to Grace Cathedral, as I am without a car."

I was delighted. It was an opportunity to know this man in a more personal way, and I welcomed it. I don't remember what we talked about on that first day. I just remember feeling totally at ease with him in a steady stream of conversational interchange. He was charming and I was charmed.

When we arrived at Grace Cathedral, he asked me if I had ever seen the building. I had not, so he insisted on giving me a quick tour. He led me here and there, pointing out stained glass windows he had helped design and murals that decorated the walls. With obvious delight and affection, he showed me through the whole Cathedral, pouring out his enthusiasm in a gush of energy—and in a hurry. I was to discover he was almost always in a hurry.

As we rushed through the Cathedral, two visiting Roman Catholic priests spotted "the Bishop." They introduced themselves, kissing his bishop's ring out of respect. *How foreign that seems,* I thought to myself. Rituals were not a part of my background.

Then suddenly he was off—to his office, or a meeting, or somewhere. "Thank you for the ride," he called over his shoulder.

Being with Bishop Pike was much like being touched by a whirlwind. I was excited and delighted. What a way to start a summer school session!

On Thursday I went back to class with new interest, but with no thought that my encounter with "the Bishop" had been anything more than a delightful incident. At the first break in our morning class, however, Bishop Pike rushed down the aisle to where I was sitting and said, "I want to thank you again for giving me a ride to the Cathedral on Tuesday. I'd like to repay you by taking you to lunch."

I was absolutely astonished by his attention and his invitation. Rather breathlessly, I thanked him and said I would be delighted.

We did not exactly have a personal or intimate sharing over lunch, since by the time we reached the restaurant, a whole collection of other students had joined us. Lunch turned out to be a kind of miniseminar. But that, too, I came to learn, was part of his life-style. He had very little time to himself. He was a very public person.

As I left the school that day, Bishop Pike scampered to catch up with me, calling out for me to wait. He said he was sorry he was driving his own car that day—he would rather ride with me. I laughed and said he would be welcome.

I drove away, flushed and warm-feeling, wondering at his attention. Suddenly I heard a honk. He pulled alongside me in his car and waved, flashing a warm smile. Then he passed me and was gone.

He likes me, I registered in astonishment. I knew he would not bring his own car again.

A Marriage "Made in Heaven"

The next week, Jim spoke to me at the lunch break. "I am in need of a ride again today. Can you take me back to the Cathedral?" He said it casually, as though it were only a coincidence. I sensed he had worked it out that way.

"Of course," I answered softly.

His lecture in the theology class had been on "Peak Experiences" that day, and as we drove away in my car, I shared with him my delight that he had acknowledged the importance of transcendent experiences of direct knowing in a class on theology. We began to share events from our own lives which fitted the category, and I sensed a direct line of communication which went beyond, or beneath, the words we were speaking.

Suddenly I thought to myself, *I am already married to this man!* As the words formed in my mind, I "saw" a relationship—an energy bond of oneness—descend on us as though from "above." So strong was my sense of union with him that I felt that to touch Jim would be to have intercourse with him. It was as though intimacy were already a fact, so complete was our "marriage" in that moment.

I said nothing to him about the experience when it happened. It was so strange to me. I hardly knew the man, and I knew nothing of his personal life or his relationship with his wife. What could possibly have prompted such a thought and experience? As though from the same "place" of knowing, the thought came in: *Perhaps we were married in another lifetime.*

I did not even believe in reincarnation then, so the second thought was as disconcerting as the first. But during the months ahead, as Jim and I became acquainted, we both kept feeling we already knew everything there was to know about each other, even though on a conscious plane we did not. There was no need for us to "develop" a relationship; from the very first we were extraordinarily compatible and at ease

24

with each other. It seemed all we had to do was to "embrace" the marriage that was already ours, to decide whether or not to live in it and manifest it fully.

A Decision to Receive the Gift

My crisis over that decision came early. After the summer school classes ended and Jim and I had our fifth and last ride across the bridge, I knew I would hear from him again. So I put the question to myself: *Do I want to enter this relationship and live it out?* I made a list of pros and cons. The cons outnumbered the pros, but when it came to the weight and importance of each item, the balance shifted the other way:

Jim was a married man. He had been separated from his wife for over a year, but they were not divorced. Therefore, to realize *my* relationship with him meant—according to the value system of my Protestant ethic and family upbringing—to "have an affair" with him. Since I was on the staff of a church and working with youth and children, I knew there was great potential for scandal and offense in such an arrangement. I had no intention of being dishonest or deceptive if I chose the relationship—discreet, yes, but not dishonest—so I felt I needed to consider the possibility that I might be dismissed from my church job "in disgrace" if our "affair" were to come to light publicly.

Moreover, there was my family to take into account. We were very close, and I knew that their love for me was unconditional. Yet to ask them to accept a relationship so contrary to their own values was to ask much—perhaps too much. Jim was my parents' age—only a year younger than my mother and two years younger than my dad—and he was "famous" and "controversial." "Famous" was a word that translated in feeling tone to "infamous" in my childhood sense of things, for one of the things most to be avoided in our little Nebraska hometown had been having people "talk about" you. "What will other people think?" had been a guideline for conduct in my growing years, and I knew that not all my family's friends nor our relatives would "think well" of Jim. Would my parents be willing to absorb all of that into their own lives, or would choosing Jim mean giving up my family?

So went my thinking about the cons. On the other hand, there was the overwhelming sense that this relationship was not only right and meant to be but already was. Not to receive the gift of such a "marriage made in heaven" would be, I felt, to deny that inner sense I had so long nurtured that there was "a man" out there somewhere with whom I could totally share my life. Here he was. How could I say "no" to him?

I took a deep breath and decided to embrace the relationship as it was given to me—however it might unfold.

Sharing Our Union

Only two days after Brad left California to return to New York, I had a phone call from Jim. He was coming to Palo Alto for a baptism and wondered if I would meet him in San Francisco for lunch and then drive him to the baptism. I agreed.

Thus began a year-long series of periodic meetings in which Jim and I shared what time we could find together. He was by then living in Santa Barbara and traveling all over the country lecturing and giving sermons. His travels brought him to the San Francisco Bay area an average of once every two weeks. When he was there, I would pick him up at the end of his event or meet him at the airport hotel where he was staying. For the most part, our "visiting" took place from 11 P.M. until 4 or so in the morning. Then he would fly away again at 8 A.M. till the next time.

I was a virgin when I met Jim. I had not wanted to be sexually intimate with someone unless it was an expression of giving myself totally to the person and the relationship. I had been reconsidering this value at the time we met, wondering if it made sense to deny myself "sexual fulfillment" when I might never find someone to whom I would choose to give my whole self. After I met Jim, I was glad I had waited.

It was a surprise to me how totally natural it was to have intercourse with him. It did not happen, as I had sensed that day in the car, the first time we touched. In fact, the first time Jim touched me was on the last day of classes. As he got out of the car, he took my hand in his, kissed it, and said, "I'd like to see you again." I said I would like that, too.

On the day of the baptism, he greeted me with a kiss and held my hand as we walked to the car after lunch. I felt like a schoolgirl with a crush. Later that afternoon he kissed me again, but only briefly.

It was on the next occasion of our meeting that we were first intimate. I went to have lunch with him at his hotel. As we shared, I felt such an intense drawing to him I could hardly breathe, let alone eat. I knew if he touched me, I would make love with him. He did, I did, we did.

It was magnificent, natural, joyful, satisfying. As we lay side by side sharing, in the late afternoon of that beautiful sun-filled Sunday, I told Jim I had never before been intimate with anyone. He was astonished, delighted, incredulous. Our "union" was fresh, pure, and perfect.

Wrestling with Priorities

It was strange how all questions of morality and immorality faded in the light of real love. There could be nothing "wrong" with such giving of self to another. It was beautiful and pure. I had no sense of "sinning." I knew if I ever had to speak publicly in the Church or elsewhere about Jim's and my "affair," I would not hesitate to testify to its wholesomeness and "rightness." Perfect love casts out all fear, and any fear I might have had of criticism or nonacceptance fell away in the light of my profound experience of full human love.

The second time we were intimate, I spent the night with Jim and discovered a whole new dimension of intimacy. There

27

was a communion between our bodies and our beings that went on even when we were asleep. That communion was the experience of our being indeed one.

The next time we were together, I found myself falling in love with him. This was different from *being* in love, or just plain loving. It had to do with "falling into" an energy of romantic illusion that made it impossible for me to concentrate on other aspects of my life. It had to do with allowing the energies of sexual attraction to take over and dominate instead of being the vehicle of expression for higher love energies. My thoughts constantly wandered to Jim. He was becoming the center of my life.

I knew I would not allow that to happen. My life had always been centered in God. To put another person at the center would be a denial of all I had chosen for myself up to that point. It would throw everything out of balance in my life.

I wrote Jim a long letter, telling him I could not see him anymore and explaining why. Then I entered an intense period of inner struggle. I experienced it as a wrestling with the devil—with that temptation to put a man, a person, at the heart of my life and the center of my being, instead of God himself. I did not choose to live that way; yet I loved Jim more profoundly than anyone else I had ever met.

In the midst of my struggle, I heard from Jim by phone. He acknowledged my letter and said that, though he was very sorry, he respected my decision and would not try to change my mind. This was a great gift of freedom to me. Now the struggle was clearly and solely my own—an internal wrestling with the major priorities of my life.

The turning point came one Wednesday afternoon. It was my day off, and I had gone for a drive in the hills. Surrounded and filled with a strong sense of my Oneness with All That Is—that is, with God—I suddenly heard myself affirming aloud that I did not *need* a man in my life, that I did not *need* a sexual relationship, that I did not *want* anything more than my Oneness with God. I felt as though I were taking a vow of celibacy, and it felt good and right. My priorities were straight once again. I was "safe and clear" in the most severe struggle with temptation I had faced until that point in my life.

Monotheistic Marriage

The next day Jim called, after a silence of several weeks. Would I have dinner with him Saturday evening? he asked. He just wanted to see me and talk with me. I checked within and felt and saw nothing but clarity. I agreed to meet him, knowing that he no longer represented any threat to my spiritual being.

We had a long talk that evening. I shared with Jim what my struggle had been about. To my amazement, he understood. "Of course," he acknowledged. "The problem of idolatry. That would be a mistake for either of us. But you could not put me at the center of your life any more than I could you. 'Hear O Israel, the Lord thy God is *one* God and thou shalt have no other gods before Him.' That is the great commandment in the light of which all other ethical claims fall into their proper places. Neither of us could live any differently."

So profound was our sharing that I re-entered the fullness of our union, in joy and thanksgiving. As we gave ourselves to each other that evening, I experienced the ecstasy of spiritual union in cosmic awareness in the midst of our physical orgasm. I knew not only oneness with Jim in those moments but full consciousness of my Oneness with All That Is at the same time. We were part of a monotheistic "marriage," and it was magnificent, free, and light-filled.

I found a new meaning for chastity in that experience. I realized that chastity has to do with purity of heart, not solely with refraining from sexual intercourse. It is in the *heart* where impurities lie, even if we restrain physically from expressing them.

29

On the other hand, if God is *by choice* at the conscious center of our lives, then we cannot, do not, will not adulterate our own divine beings. My love for Jim was pure, and free from any desire to "have him" for myself, to cling to him, to "keep him." He did not "belong to me," for we both belonged to God.

For the rest of that year, when we were separated far more than we were together, I practiced a "ritual" of nonattachment. After each visit with Jim, I would go home and "let him go" completely. I would consciously release him to the universe, to God, giving thanks for all we had thus far shared and leaving the future entirely in "God's hands." I would let go of any *expectations* that I would ever hear from him or see him again, in order to live in a state of *abundant expectancy* instead. I later came to recognize *having no expectations* as one of the basic principles of higher consciousness living, and I was grateful I had begun to practice it early in my life experience.

Sometimes I wept during that releasing. It was like grieving for the "end" of the relationship, even though there was always the chance—even the probability—that it would go on. Sometimes it took a few hours to let go completely. Sometimes it would take me as long as three days. But when it was done, I would turn my full attention to my life as it was going on, and I would rejoice in that.

I considered the "ritual" a self-discipline in nonidolatrous relating during that year. And it was that. I look back on it now also as a rehearsal for the great releasing and letting go that was to come during grief, and I am grateful for that year of consciously chosen preparation.

Uniting Our Professional Lives

After a full year in which we enjoyed our "marriage" while basically separated from each other by time and space, an opportunity opened up for me to move to Santa Barbara to work with Jim. I felt my decision had to be based on motivations other than the desire to be near Jim, for I did not want to form attachments to him or to develop expectations of him or of our relationship which would in any way limit, restrict, or weigh down the joyful union we already shared. So, on the merits of the professional contacts that would open up for me an entirely new world—that of writing, publishing, and lecturing—I agreed to be the executive director of a small literary foundation Jim had established, and moved to Santa Barbara.

Within just weeks of my assuming that post, I was thrust with Jim into a study of psychic phenomena as a result of enormous public response to Jim's revelation that he believed he had been able, with the aid of three different mediums, to communicate with his son, Jim, Jr., after his son's death by suicide. Before long, Jim and I were writing a book together about his psychic experiences. It was soon published under the title *The Other Side*.*

We were as compatible in our professional life and work as we were personally, and during the second year of our "marriage," we managed to be together almost constantly. We lived together, traveled together, wrote together, studied together. We were one.

Both of us were astonished that we did not feel the need for "time alone"—that is, time apart from each other. We were not only *content* to be together twenty-four hours a day, we preferred it. Again, there was no "growth" involved in our relationship. It had been, as we experienced it, full-blown from its very beginning. We were simply enjoying the fruits of a union that seemed to have been given as a gift.

Marriage "in the Church"

As we entered our third year of life together, we began to talk of marriage in the conventional sense. Jim's wife, Esther, had filed for divorce a year before and the decree was now

* By James A. Pike with Diane Kennedy, New York: Doubleday & Co., 1968.

final. It seemed only fitting that we should have our "marriage" recognized legally by the state and blessed by the Church. It was in relation to the latter that Jim's crisis over the choosing of our relationship set in.

Never in the history of the Christian Church (!) had a bishop divorced and remarried. Although the Canon Law of the Episcopal Church allowed for the divorce and remarriage of clergy and made no exception of bishops, divorce was unprecedented for a bishop and therefore bound to cause great controversy within the Episcopal Church and beyond.

Jim chose to go ahead, however, and began to lay carefully the foundation for our request to be granted permission to be married in the Church. It seemed one thing in our favor was that the bishop whose permission we needed was one of Jim's longest-standing friends in the priesthood. At first Bishop Kim Myers indicated there would be no problem as far as he was concerned. Then—for reasons that remain unknown to me—he changed his mind and decided Jim would have to offer some "proof" of his emotional and psychological stability.

There followed a long series of "letters of proof," psychological interviews, and conversations with Bishop Myers. At length, Bishop Myers declared Jim's marriage with Esther "dead," which was all the canonical clearance we needed to be married, but said he could not give his personal blessing to our union.

We were sorry—we had asked Kim to perform the ceremony—but we did not feel that his refusal to give his own approval was critical. Only *after* the wedding did we realize how important Kim felt his blessing to be.

Two days after we celebrated our union, with four ministers officiating and some sixty close friends and family as witnesses, Bishop Myers sent out a personal letter to all the priests in his diocese and to all his brother bishops, saying that he had not approved of our wedding and asking that they no longer invite Jim to perform any priestly functions under their auspices. The result was an almost universally effective "gentleman's agreement" to ban Jim from the Church. The impact on Jim was profound. He felt that his priesthood had been voided by his friend's personal request, and he refused to carry a title under which he could not function. He felt that his only choice was to leave the Church, since there was no other way for him to renounce his title.

Our New Ministry

Thus in the spring of 1969, Jim announced his intention to "abandon the communion" of the Episcopal Church, and he and I began to build a new life and ministry for ourselves. We set up a nonprofit foundation to minister to the needs of persons like ourselves who were "church alumni" or just on the inside edge of the Church—persons who were restless with institutional religion for whatever reason but who still sought to be faithful to their covenant with God. We wanted to help such persons to live out their faith in the context of secular society.

As we launched our new Foundation for Religious Transition, Jim moved into a sense of even greater urgency than before. He had always seemed in a hurry—involved in a myriad of activities and projects at once. Now he pressed himself even harder. We lived fully—so fully that friends and family said that our visits were like hurricanes of energy swirling in and out of their life-spaces. We traveled a lot, had visitors in our home on all but three nights of the eight months we lived there, accomplished a great deal of research into the origins of Christianity and writing in preparation for our next book, which was to be an historical life of Jesus, and relished every moment we shared.

We both had a feeling for leaving nothing unsaid or unexpressed, even for a matter of hours. There is a Biblical adage that says, "Do not let the sun go down on your anger." We determined that we would not let it set on *any* feeling or thought between us. We liked being totally up to date.

We talked of the future—of life and death—but primarily we were focused intently on living the present moment to the fullest. It was as though we were cramming a lifetime of living into three short years.

And so it turned out to be.

2

SHOCK SETS IN
Death in the Desert

JIM AND I had flown to Israel, where we intended to begin writing the manuscript of the book on the historical Jesus which was to culminate three years of research for Jim and two for me. In order to put ourselves more fully in touch with the inner meaning of some of the events in Jesus' life, we planned to spend leisurely time in several key locales. One of these was the wilderness of Judea where the Gospels say Jesus spent forty days and nights fasting, praying, and being tempted by the devil.

At noon on Monday, September 1, 1969, Jim and I got into our rented car and set out for the wilderness of Judea. It was an insufferably hot Middle Eastern day. Temperatures had risen to about 140 degrees Fahrenheit. We were in the midst of a major heat wave, which was scheduled to last for days—perhaps even weeks. Jim and I determined to go anyway. We wanted to get a firsthand feeling for the desert area in which Jesus was tempted and won his inner battle.

We each completed that journey alone. Jim in his way. I in mine. Our car got stuck in a deep rut, and we tried to walk out together. We had no water to drink, our clothing was inadequate to protect us from the sun, we had little knowledge of desert survival, and an erroneous sense of direction had us traveling in nearly the opposite direction from what we intended.

After four hours we both collapsed in exhaustion. Jim felt he had to sleep. I felt we had to press on. After resting for some time, I left Jim to go for help. I struggled for ten long hours in a severe canyon and on hills and cliffs before I finally found someone. Then, with only a few hours' restless interim, filled with the deepest anxiety for Jim's life, I took a police search party back to the place where I had left Jim. We did not find him there.

I had been in the desert for more than twenty-four hours in temperatures ranging from 130 to 145 degrees. I was exhausted, and I was sure Jim was dead. This was the beginning of the first stage of grief for me. I was on the verge of entering shock.

It was then that my first great learning came. I discovered enormous strength in myself which I had never had occasion to call on before. It was a deep, inner, spiritual strength that saw me through the first hours, days, and weeks of grief. It was a strength that gave me clarity of mind, so I could act quickly and efficiently and do what needed to be done, a strength that dulled my sensitivity to my feelings, so I would not be handicapped by pain. It was a strength that surged upward in my being in response to a crisis and saw me through it in loving care and guidance. It was a strength that protected me through shock. It was my Higher Self in action.

That deep strength is in each and all of us, but most of us do not call on it until we are in circumstances of dire need. Then its ministry to us seems almost miraculous and others often look on us in admiration and disbelief. "She is holding up so well," people say in wonder. "Where does she get her strength?" The answer is "From her Higher Self," but often we are not aware of the source at the time we actually draw on the strength.

Most of us are not aware that we are in shock until we come out of it, and so it was with me. But, in retrospect, I recognized the gift that my Higher Self—that aspect of my being that knows what is best for me, what is in harmony with the larger Plan—had been giving me from the very beginning.

From Hysteria to Shock

The police drove me to our hotel at the end of the first long day of searching for Jim.* We had not found him where I left him, and prospects that we would find him alive were not good. Shocks went through my body as I saw on the streets one man after another who appeared to be Jim. It was as though my Little Self—that deep-feeling child within me—was hoping against all hope for a miracle: that Jim was in Jerusalem, alive and well, walking along the street unconcerned. The disappointment and pain my Little Self suffered each time we got close enough to see that it was not Jim were almost unbearable.

Back at the hotel, I went to our room alone. The first thing I saw as I entered the room was a huge bouquet of flowers. Immediately I thought of a funeral, and the scent of the flowers made me sick to my stomach. I picked up the vase, removed the card without looking at it, and took the flowers to the door, where I planned to set them outside.

The man who worked on that floor was standing there. He said, "Do you not want them, madam?" "No, please," I said almost desperately, thrusting them into his hands. (It turned out that the flowers were actually sent by the travel agency that had handled our reservations, as a welcome to Israel to Jim and me. Their arrival at a time more appropriate for condolences was purely coincidental.)

I closed the door again and collapsed in tears. The tears, once released, very quickly grew into hysteria. My Little Self,

* For the full story of the events of that week, see *Search*, by Diane Kennedy Pike, New York: Doubleday, 1970, and Pocket Books, 1971.

through which all my feelings flow, began to shriek and shout, striking out with her words at the walls and at the world, and with her fists at the bed.

I wandered about the room almost as an automaton. My body was trembling all over and covered with cold perspiration. Suddenly my mind interrupted with an important thought: *You should call home before Jim's mother* [who was eighty-four] *hears the news on the radio or television. The shock would be more than she could bear.*

My Little Self and my body ceased their hysteria. Higher Self—who was observing the whole process—took control and put in a call to California, to my parents' home. My mind very efficiently figured out for me that it would be 9:45 A.M. in San Jose and that my mother would be home alone. Little Self felt bad about breaking this news to her while she was alone, but Higher Self saw no better alternative and knew it would be O.K.

While I waited for the call to go through, my mind recalled something else for me. Jim and I had made a dinner date for that evening. With studied composure, I called Professor Shlomo Pines of the Hebrew University and told him what had happened, maintaining Higher Self control only with great exertion of effort.

Back to the hysteria—shouting, crying, pacing. The phone rang. Instantly, Higher Self took charge again and talked to the operator. Then Mother's voice was on the line. Suddenly, Little Self was talking with her mother, sobbing out her story—a child whose heart had been broken.

The emotional trauma of that telephone conversation was so intense for my Little Self that it was not until six years after Jim's death that I was able to fully recall what we had said. Little Self had not been ready for a total replay of, and release from, that scene until she had dealt with all the other hurt she had suffered. In those moments, as she shared with her mother the deepest pain she had yet suffered in this lifetime, she laid herself completely open and bare. She felt totally safe in her mother's "arms," and her raw wounds of pure grief lay open and unprotected.

Mother says we talked for at least forty-five minutes. I began by saying—with high tension in my voice—"Something terrible has happened. Jim is dead!" Then I told Mother the entire story. I remember shrieking (or so it felt to Little Self, who was crying helplessly), "He wasn't there! We couldn't find him! He was nowhere to be found!!" Over and over again I poured out my pain to my mother.

Somehow my mind managed to get in a reminder about Jim's mother, and Little Self relayed the message frantically about getting to her and the rest of Jim's and my family before the news broke in the media. Little Self had fully accepted my mind's projection that to hear the news without preparation would be too much for Jim's mother, and Little Self felt an urgency about passing along my mind's suggestion of friends who could go to be with Pearl when they told her the news.

Then my Little Self heard a loving mother expressing concern for her: Was I alone? Should she and Dad come to Israel to be with me? Had I seen a doctor? *See* a doctor. Have him give me something to help me sleep.

Little Self responded with grateful obedience. My mind had not thought of a doctor, and the question of sleep had not yet come up. Little Self was surprised at my mother's concern for me, because all her energies had been focused on Jim. She was grateful.

When I hung up, Little Self re-entered her hysteria. She tore her clothing off, throwing it in the wastebasket, feeling she would never again have the strength to wash or mend clothes. To remove each item was a terrific drain of energy. My sandals were stuck to my bloodied, blistered feet and had to be torn off.

Little Self kept shouting, Why did I leave him? *Why* didn't I stay to die with him in the desert? My God, I left him all *alone* in the desert. I would rather have died there. Then

39

she would lash out: How could such a thing happen? It can't be. It just can't be! And, I got out and got help, but *we couldn't find him!!*

Frustration, distress, disbelief, anger, despair, agony, confusion—all of these emotions flooded my being, making it difficult for Higher Self to maintain any semblance of control.

But Higher Self was watching and observing dispassionately, wisely. In time Higher Self said to Little Self, gently, *You are hysterical. Your body is trembling all over. Go stand under the shower and calm down.* My Little Self responded obediently, and as the water washed over my body, it stopped trembling and Little Self stopped crying.

My mind, registering the bruises and cuts and blisters that covered my whole body, reminded Little Self of Mother's suggestion that I see a doctor. Little Self agreed it was a good idea.

It must have been then, or shortly thereafter, that I went into shock. The doctor gave me some kind of tranquilizer, and that must have helped put Little Self into a state of numbness. I called my family again after returning from the doctor's, and they later told me my voice had settled into a high, level tone, where it stayed pitched for weeks until I finally came out of shock.

Shock is the first stage of grief for nearly everyone. Sometimes it occurs *before* the physical death of the loved one, when a severe illness or accident forewarns almost certain death. Usually it follows learning that the person has in fact died.

Surely each of us responds differently when face to face with a loved one's transition through death, and the circumstances surrounding the event must make a big difference. Yet the overall patterns of reaction and response seem to be the same,* and shock nearly always sets in for a time even when one has been prepared for and expects the death.

* See *Up from Grief: Patterns of Recovery*, by Bernadine Kreis and Alice Pattie, New York: The Seabury Press, 1969.

Shock was a totally new experience for me. It is one I am grateful to have had, for through it I learned so much about my internal functionings. I came to trust my inner processes and my Higher Self's direction of my life more fully, perhaps, through grief than through any other life experience.

Higher Self in Control

For the rest of the week, while the police searched for Jim, my body and Little Self were almost completely numb. They felt little and reacted to little. Sometimes—as when the word came that they had found Jim's body—I could literally feel more numbness flood through my being as though to prevent Little Self from feeling, so that I could keep functioning. I was not on any kind of tranquilizer. Shock was like having natural injections of anesthesia permeate my system.

Because the dulling of my emotional response was natural, my mind was able to continue to function in total alertness. It faithfully recorded every detail of what transpired during that week—that is, every detail of what my attention was focused on.

And Higher Self was clearly in charge.

On the first day, before I went into shock, I had returned with the police to the canyon area where I had left Jim. My mind had observed—objectively, I suppose, considering the data it had to draw on as I looked over the canyon area in which Jim and I had gotten lost—*What a desolate place!* Even then Higher Self had responded at once, *Barren, yes. Forbidding. But not desolate. It is filled with a strange beauty, and it inspires courage and strength. It is filled with the power of God.*

It was also on that very first day of the search (before shock) that my mind was panicking Little Self with observations such as: *They'll never find Jim. The canyon is too deep. There are too many caves.* Or, *He must be dead by now.* Yet Higher Self was saying, *This is all part of a pattern. Though it is hard to see how or why, everything is happening just as it*

41

was meant to. This is part of a larger plan. Everything is as it should be.

After I went into shock, Higher Self was even more fully in control. Since Little Self was not feeling much, it was far easier for Higher Self to direct my mind and keep it under control as well. As I went back to the desert with the searchers, sat in the police major's office, talked to representatives of the press, told the story to my brother Scott (who had come from the States to be with me), waited endless hours for word from the search parties, answered phone calls from the States, Higher Self monitored everything. Little Self and my body were like obedient children, dipping into their pain only infrequently and slightly, and using most of their energy to do what was at hand in every situation. Sometimes Little Self would say, *I can't go on.* Higher Self would respond lovingly, *Of course not. But you're not in charge now, I am. We can make it.*

Because Higher Self was in charge, I lived in an almost perpetual state of meditation and prayer. I felt for the first three days of the search that Jim was living on, or sharing, my physical energy. I concentrated on that energy flow, out of my heart center to Jim's. I rested and ate, though very little, primarily with Jim in mind. *He needs your strength,* Higher Self kept reminding my body.

On Friday afternoon, I felt a change take place. Though I was still channeling energy to Jim, I suddenly felt he was no longer receiving it. That cutoff came at about 2 P.M. on September 5.

I feel now, in my deepest inner self, that it was at about 2 P.M. on that Friday that Jim broke free of his physical body. There are many who say that most persons require from three to ten days to sever the energy cord that connects the flow of the Life Energy with the physical body. In a natural death, this separation takes place during the final days and hours of "dying." In the case of sudden death, the separation takes place after the physiological processes of life have ceased. The desert decays bodies with extraordinary rapidity, so it is entirely possible that Jim died around noon on Tuesday, the second of September, when a strong wave of panic and a certainty that Jim was dead came over me (this was before I went into shock). In the interim—between Tuesday around noon and Friday about 2 P.M.—he might indeed have drawn on my physical energy to sustain his energy body until he was reoriented enough to make the transition of leaving his physical body altogether. The autopsy (performed on Sunday, September 7) confirmed that the corpse had been dead from five to ten days. It had been six days since we had left to go into the desert, and five since the first day of the search.

My inner feeling was also reinforced by the transcript of a mediumistic sitting held in London on the Thursday evening of the search for Jim. The medium was apparently able to make contact with Jim—that is, to register the frequencies of his consciousness at that time. He "reported" being in a state of confusion, knowing his body was dead but not being able to move on because he could not see clearly. His eyes were clouded over, he said, and he was waiting for someone to come and show him the way. As I see it, he was able to break free and move on less than twenty-four hours later.

"Jim," Speaking Through Mrs. Twigg

Because so many people have asked about my experiences of mediumistic communication with Jim since his death, I share here my comments on that sitting. John Pearce-Higgins, a priest-friend of Jim's in London and the person who had introduced Jim to the medium Ena Twigg,* in 1966, was contacted by Mrs. Twigg to see if he would help her try to contact Jim's

---

* See *The Other Side*, by James A. Pike with Diane Kennedy, New York: Doubleday & Co., 1968, and New York: Dell Paperback, 1969; and *Ena Twigg: Medium*, by Ena Twigg with Ruth Hagy Brod, New York: Hawthorn Books, Inc., 1972.

deceased son, Jim, Jr. It had been their hope (as it was all of ours) that Jim (Sr.) was still alive and that Mrs. Twigg would be able to help the searchers locate him through the cooperation of Jim, Jr., from the "other side," a way of referring to ongoing life after the transition of death. Mrs. Twigg had thus far in the week been unable to reach Jim, Jr., and had on Wednesday begun to feel enveloped in a gray mist whenever she turned her attention to either of the Jims.

I offer here the substance of their sitting, with my comments inserted throughout so that the reader might understand why I found the sitting evidential felt that it had, indeed, been my husband whom Mrs. Twigg contacted, or "registered."

In my experience, the "conversations" reported by a medium during a seance are a translation of what is actually going on. The process of reporting is very much like the one I am using in this book when I refer to internal dialogues between the various facets of myself. In actuality there are, of course, no such dialogues. There are only energy waves of different lengths and frequencies being registered in my consciousness. In order to communicate to you my understanding of those inner experiences, however, I have translated them into dialogues—a language with which you are familiar.

I feel a similar transaction takes place in genuine mediumistic transmission. The medium registers in his or her own consciousness certain energy waves. He or she then translates those impulses into words, usually in the form of a dialogue, which will convey to the sitter the meaning the medium has attributed to them. Thus Mrs. Twigg reports what "Jim said," but in reality she is telling us what she understands to be happening with Jim.

I have stayed with the direct dialogue style here—again, for ease of communication—hoping that you, the reader, will remind yourself that I do not take the conversation quite as literally as it sounds.

Present at the sitting held on Thursday, September 4,

1969, beginning at 8:30 P.M. at the home of Mr. and Mrs. Harry Twigg in London, England, were Ena Twigg (the medium), Canon John D. Pearce-Higgins and Harry Twigg. They sought evidence as to the whereabouts of Jim in the desert in Israel.

Canon Pearce-Higgins opened with a prayer, during which Mrs. Twigg fell into a trance. When she began speaking, she was breathing heavily and moaning, "Oh . . . oh . . . oh . . . Help me! He-e-e-lp me!" Then she began sobbing, crying, groaning and gasping and repeated the cries for help.

Jim's last words to me as I left him there in the desert to go for help had been: "Yell 'Help me!' all the way." I had indeed done that, for six hours. When I listened to the tape of the Twigg sitting and heard that Jim's first words were "Help me," I felt certain Jim had followed his own advice. Knowing how unbelievably relieved and grateful I had been when I finally heard a response to my cries for help, I could sense what comfort there must have been for Jim finally to be able to communicate with someone. That John Pearce-Higgins was in London would not have mattered then, for Jim would no longer have been using his physical body to transmit his thoughts.

Pearce-Higgins assured "Jim" that they were trying to help him and repeated several times, "God bless you." Then he asked, "Where are you?" Jim responded that he was lost— in "a nowhere."

Not only had we been lost in the desert, but it seemed Jim was feeling "lost" in still another way. He had not been consciously prepared for death, so it must have been terribly confusing to suddenly "find" himself not only lost physically but also between two planes, or modes, of existence and states of consciousness.

Then Jim "said," "I'm in the end of the pattern . . . It had to be . . . It had to be . . ."

That it was all according to a perfect pattern was also the

message my Higher Self had begun giving me from Tuesday afternoon on. Here Jim appears to assert his own conviction of that—no doubt a message coming through to him from his Higher Self as well.

One of my most important learnings of recent years was greatly heightened by my experiences during grief. It has to do with the matter of "perfect patterns," or, as I used to call them, "God's will for our lives." What I have come to know is that there is a perfect pattern for each of our lives which, if lived out consciously and by choice, leads to great soul growth and a sense of inner peace and harmony. This pattern is not imposed on us arbitrarily, by some "outside" power or force— God, in the sense of an "other"—as is implied in the concept of fate, but rather it is the result of our past-life growth and experiences. The pattern changes as our new experiences are fed into it, and we are thus constantly altering what is "right" for our lives and what we "must" do to live in harmony with our Higher Selves.

Jim and I had made conscious choices about going out into the desert. Though we did not consciously get the car stuck, all other decisions were ours—going out there to begin with, without a guide or other third party along; not carrying water; not taking precautions, like wearing sunhats and hiking boots; deciding to walk out, and which direction to go as we started; whether to go into the canyon or stay out of it; whether to stay in one place or go on searching for help, etc., etc., etc. Therefore, there was no way that our being in the circumstances we were in could possibly be called an "accident."

And once we were face to face with death, we made choices about how to respond to that as well: we both kept going, kept choosing "life," until, in different ways, each of our struggles came to an end.

Moreover, there were the larger patterns of our lives into which this particular journey into the wilderness fitted for each of us. And there was the pattern of our life in union with each other. In all these regards, each of us had been making choices that in turn either fulfilled or altered the "perfect pattern" we had come in with at the beginning of this lifetime.

Now Jim's life in the body had ended. This was in harmony with *his* pattern. I was still alive in my body. This was according to *mine*. That our full and perfect union had lasted only three years was also part of the pattern—and how that was in perfection I came to understand only after I had finished the most painful part of my grieving.

The point, for me, is that there was no reason to blame anyone or anything "outside" us as responsible for what had happened. God, after all, is at work within us. The degree to which we are conscious of our Oneness with God is the degree to which we experience the peace and harmony of doing His Will—of living according to our perfect patterns. If we do not choose to live in that harmony, that's not God's "fault."

There were many who said to me after Jim's death that God must have had great plans for me or I would not have been spared, or saved. Implicit in this for me was that God had *not* had great plans for Jim because he had *not* survived. I could not affirm either side of that proposition.

Others said, "Do you feel Jim chose to die there?" On the one hand I could say "yes," in that Jim had certainly chosen to *go* there, where he died. On the other hand, I had to say "no," for he had not chosen to go there *to die*, but rather as one expression of his ongoing life-quest.

What I *do* affirm is that we were conscious participants in the forming of our destinies and that no aspect of our lives could be in any sense considered a "mere accident." An event as large as death is always an expression of the life (or lives) lived up to that point, I feel. When two persons are in a state of joyous harmony and peace as they approach "death," as we were, surely the death itself is an expression of harmony and therefore is in perfection.

As the "conversation" went on, Jim said, "I'm not a

47

coward . . . not . . . not dead, John." Pearce-Higgins responded, "Are you dead?" The answer came back, "Dead . . . Yes, I'm nowhere."

Here is reflected the confusion of our language. Jim was "dead," yet not "dead," else how could he be communicating with John?

The "conversation" went on, with attempts by John Pearce-Higgins to reassure Jim and give him some orientation regarding his state of being. Jim is then quoted as saying, "If I believed before, then now I must believe even more," and, "I had to die to prove it was true to the others . . ."

These comments I feel to have come primarily from the mind of the medium. I have heard the phrases in other sittings, and I know that whereas Mrs. Twigg's entire life's work is focused on assuring people—indeed, proving to people—that their loved ones live on, and that there *is* a life after death, that was *not* a primary interest or concern of Jim's. Often what is in the mind of the medium seeps through, I feel, and gets intertwined with thoughts being transmitted from another focus of consciousness—in this case, Jim, it would seem.

In response to Canon Pearce-Higgins' question as to what happened to him, Jim said at length, "Choked . . . choked . . ."

The police explained to me, before I identified Jim's body, what the process of dying by dehydration in the sun is like. One of the things they said was that, in the end, you *choke* to death, because the tongue swells up and fills your throat and you can no longer breathe. Jim seemed to confirm that experience.

Then Jim said, "She went . . . loving me, John," and, "They'll lose my ring, won't they? They'll lose my ring . . ."

As I left Jim that Monday afternoon, I said, "If I die along the way, you'll know I went because I love you." Here Jim seemed to be referring to that remark, to that understanding between us.

48

His repeated references to his ring were among the most evidential aspects of the sitting for me, for when I identified Jim's body (and, of course, long before I heard the tape of this session), I asked, without *any* prior thought, for Jim's wedding ring. They told me that the coroner would remove the personal effects and return them to me. When we went to receive the autopsy and to pick up the personal effects, I felt an inner *demand* to get Jim's ring. I could hardly wait for the doctor to finish his report on the autopsy before I said, "May I have his ring, please?" I was almost embarrassed at the urgency I felt. The doctor handed me a small plastic bag. I thanked him, went at once to the lavatory, removed Jim's ring, rinsed the formaldehyde off it, and slipped it on my left ring finger with my own wedding ring. When I had done so, a wave of relief swept over me.

I could not understand this experience at the time, though Scott kept assuring me it was all right for me to want to have Jim's ring. I am grateful to Scott for, in effect, giving me "permission" to follow my inner feelings even though he didn't know why I was feeling the way I was. Such gifts of affirmation while persons are in grief are extremely important, for they enable the one who grieves to go through his or her *own process* of grief and not be deflected from it.

When I heard the tape of the sitting, I felt sure that I had felt that sense of urgency about the ring because, for whatever reason, Jim had focused *his* attention on it. John Pearce-Higgins and Ena Twigg assumed that the references had to do with Jim's bishop's ring, but he hadn't even been wearing that. If anything, that their thoughts were running in a different vein makes Jim's words and my experience seem even more evidential. It was almost as if Jim wanted to give me a sign or a token of his love from beyond the death of his physical body. The wedding ring was it. I still wear it on my right ring finger.

In the rather lengthy "conversation" which followed,

John Pearce-Higgins tried repeatedly to get more information about the death itself. All Jim seemed able to tell him was that he had choked—not *on* anything, just "with" his throat. Neither John *nor* Jim seemed to grasp the significance of that or in any way to relate it to dehydration, but for that very reason *I* found the references to choking convincing.

Other references could have been evidential—but could also have been "good guesses" by the medium. There were, for instance, references to our "hopes." He had no doubt been sustained by his hopes that he would find me and/or help before he died, and perhaps he also sensed that *I* had been and was being sustained on *my* hopes during the entire time of my struggle to find help and our search for him. And then, too, there had been our mutual hopes for the work we were doing together through the new Foundation for Religious Transition, our writing, etc.

In addition, he referred to "my darling," which happened to be one of Jim's few pet names for me. When I first heard the taped recording of the seance, that little phrase moved me deeply. It was so like Jim to have used it. Now, as I look back with more objectivity, I can see that the phrase could have been chosen by the medium without knowing it would be so precisely right.

There followed some remarks which struck a deep chord in me. First of all, Jim said there was a strange way in which he had asked for the circumstances he found himself in—but, he said, "I didn't want this . . . through a confusion . . ."

Jim had talked since April of that year of his inner sense that he would have a major breakthrough during our trip to Israel that September. We had planned to take time in the desert, at Masada and in Galilee, just to "be," because he was so certain the breakthrough would come. Both he and I thought it would be of a spiritual or mystical type—a breakthrough to the Christ-light within. That the breakthrough came in the form of death of the physical body was not according to either of our expectations, thus catching us both off guard. But it did, in fact, happen. So it seems he sensed he *had* asked for the breakthrough, but he had not wanted it like this. He felt there had been a "confusion." Perhaps more to the point is that, had we known the *nature* of the breakthrough that was to come, both he and I might have sought to prevent it. Yet, both he *and* I were "ready" for this experience or else we wouldn't have been having it. By our not knowing in advance what was to come, the perfect pattern for Jim's death in this lifetime could be fulfilled without undue delay.

Jim seemed to be confused about what he called the "mist" he was in, and the fact that he couldn't see. He kept asking why no one had come to show him the way. John Pearce-Higgins tried to help him by explaining what he called the "River of Death" that we all have to go through. Then he spoke of the three-day period it takes most people to make the transition from "life" to life on the Other Side, the transition being what we call "death." And finally he mentioned the "vehicle of vitality" with which Jim was probably still surrounded and which would create illusions in his mind.

None of these references seemed to mean much to Jim. Apparently he was unable to understand the circumstances in which he found himself, and as a result was feeling lost and confused.

I have read reports of mediumistic communications and of persons who have been technically dead for a time and then have revived which seem to indicate that ideas and concepts we hold about life after death often lead to confusion in the actual experience of death. If "mist" was not something Jim expected, then experiencing it might have made him feel he somehow didn't measure up, or wasn't "good enough," to see things clearly.

His questions as to why "they" would do this *to him* seem to reveal old beliefs in and concepts of punishment. He later asked specifically if he was in hell, only to be reassured again by John that he was only in the mist during the transition.

At one point Jim said he didn't think they would find

what was left of him. John Pearce-Higgins asked if the Arabs got it. Jim replied, "No, the sand got it."

That was an odd reference, as there is no sand in the desert we were in—only clay that is baked to rock-hardness by the sun and dryness. Perhaps he meant to say the "desert" got it, and "desert" was "translated" into "sand." The question Pearce-Higgins asked about the Arabs was one of the speculations going around during that week of the search. I knew there were no Arabs out in that area to "get" him, but persons in other parts of the world had no way of knowing. Jim here seems to confirm the real nature of his experience.

When Canon Pearce-Higgins asked if Jim choked on the sand, Jim said he didn't know. All he knew was that he had choked.

Later he said he could not sleep because "They keep calling me." Pearce-Higgins asked, "Who keeps calling you?" Jim replied, "All of the people."

I feel sure this "calling" comprised the prayers for Jim being sent from all around the world, plus the thoughts of the many psychics and mediums who had been trying to reach him to find out where he was.

There followed a request by Jim to have "Harry give his wife to Diane for a time." Then he said it was too much to ask but he would like to see me, talk to me, when I came there and that he wanted to finish a lot of things and to put "this whole tremendous subject on the map in an academic field."

We had talked about communicating with each other when either of us died. Now perhaps Jim was feeling that Ena would be his only hope, since she was the one he reached first. Or perhaps this was the way Mrs. Twigg's eagerness to be of help was being expressed in her trance state.

As for the suggestion that Jim, because of this interest in communication from the other side, wanted to put it on the map in an academic field, this is not exactly true. Again, I feel that the medium's mind was coloring the communication. Jim had taken an interest in psychic phenomena because of his experiences of communicating with his son, and he was especially interested in the scientific research being done in the field. Psychic phenomena were *not*, however, a central interest of his, and he had no intentions of dedicating himself to research and writing in the field. However, many persons had *assumed* that this is what he intended to do, and that assumption seems to come through here, perhaps from the medium's mind.

Later he said, "Will you tell them the book must be published? . . . Not finished yet . . . but it must be published."

This must be a reference to the book on Jesus which we (Jim, my brother Scott, and I) had been working on. Scott and I did in fact finish it, and published it under the title *The Wilderness Revolt.**

After further reference to his ring and to his own frustration with his attempts to communicate, he said "Thank you" and the seance ended.†

The next day, which was Friday, Ena Twigg reported that Jim had visited her again, at eight in the evening. He told her that he had climbed up on some rocks and fallen. That he was dead.‡

That Jim had been able by Friday to "see" what had happened to him confirms my feeling that he left his body behind on that Friday afternoon around 2 P.M. Perhaps it was as his spirit rose up above his body (as I witnessed in my vision, reported below) that he "saw" for the first time where he was and what had actually happened.

---

* By Diane Kennedy Pike and R. Scott Kennedy, New York: Doubleday & Co., 1972.

† For a complete record of the seance, see *Ena Twigg: Medium, op. cit.,* pp. 180–88.

‡ *Ibid.,* p. 191.

Higher-Self Vision

One further experience that for me is evidence of the functioning of Higher Self during that week of search is the vision I had in the early morning hours of Sunday, September 7. On Saturday the search party had found the first clue, indicating they were at last on Jim's trail. I felt certain they would find him on Sunday, and of course my Little Self was hoping against all hope that he would still be found alive, in spite of the news Mrs. Twigg had given me on Friday that she was certain he was already dead. Higher Self, meanwhile, had prepared for what seemed more likely by making notes regarding preparation for a Requiem Mass and memorial service and by writing the rough draft of a statement for the press.

I continued to pray constantly for Jim. I had been eating little and sleeping even less, so it would appear that my body, mind, and Little Self were in a state of single-minded focus of the kind consciously induced by mystics seeking visionary experiences.

On Saturday I went to bed about midnight and was awakened suddenly at 1:30 A.M. by two loud knocks on the door.

I leapt out of bed and dashed to the door and flung it open. There was no one there. As I closed and locked the door and turned toward the bed again, I felt tremendously weak and dehydrated and sensed that Jim must be losing strength. I quickly got back in bed, drank a full glass of water, lay down on my back, and sent all of my energy to him, letting it flow out of me.

As I did so, I suddenly saw a very husky old woman just above the right side of my bed. My eyes were closed when I first saw her, so I opened them. She was still there.

It was not completely dark in my room, as some light came in from the outside; the front of the hotel was brightly lit. But at that moment I was aware of nothing but the darkness all around and this woman's figure. . . .

All I could see of the woman was her head, her shoulders, and her body down almost to her waist. She appeared to be dressed in some kind of loose-fitting white robe which hung in such a way as to cause the candle she was holding to cast long vertical shadows on her, giving the impression of both lightness and darkness at the same time.

Her shoulders were broad and husky, and she was carrying a very large lighted candle, the flame of which was almost directly in front of her face. The candle was so big she seemed barely able to get her hands around it. . . .

Her face was rugged-looking but kind. It was almost round, and her hair was parted in the middle and pulled back off her face, as though in a bun. She had heavy eyebrows and a very warm smile on her face.

She seemed to be approaching me quietly, slowly. Behind her was another woman in procession, approaching slowly, following as in rhythm or step with the first one. Though I had opened my eyes, I could see the woman equally well and could sense the warmth and kindness with which she approached me. Suddenly I knew she was Death.

"No!" I cried out. "Please, no!"

Immediately she disappeared, as did the figure behind her. I concentrated harder than ever before on sending my strength and energy to Jim. I knew that time was very short and he could not live much longer. I was praying desperately for his survival as I fell back to sleep.

At 3:30 A.M. I was again startled awake, this time by what seemed to be voices—not actual voices but more like those one hears in a dream. The voices were saying, almost in unison—and they seemed to be speaking from the right side of the bed, where I had seen the woman: All of the mediums say he is dying.

"No, please," I sobbed. "It's only a few hours till we will find him. Give him strength." Then as though to Jim, "Try to live, Jim. Take my strength," I called out loud.

Then I saw Jim. He was, as I saw him, lying on his left side on a ledge under a very large overhanging rock. His head was very near a crevice between the overhanging rock and one to the left of it which also bulged out but which had no ledge under it. The cliff from which the rock to the left hung seemed to jut out toward me, indicating that it sat at an angle to the ledge where I knew he was dying.

As soon as I saw Jim so clearly, I got out of bed and went into the adjoining room where Scott was asleep, because I wanted him to share that moment with me. I walked around to the right side of his bed and sat down next to him.

"Scott," I said, touching him gently to awaken him. "It's Jim. He's dying. I want you to share this with me."

Scott woke up and scooted up slightly on his pillow, not comprehending what I was saying. "It's all right," I said quietly. "It's all right."

I closed my eyes so as to see Jim better and began to describe the vision to Scott as I was seeing it.

"He's lying on a ledge," I explained, "under a large overhanging rock. It's a very smooth rock—very large. He's on his left side. I can't tell if he has a shirt on or not, but he has his trousers on and his shoes. I can tell he has his shoes on. And he is wearing his glasses. He has his glasses on.

"I can see him beginning to leave his body now," I went on, tears streaming down my face. "His spirit is very light in color— white. It seems to be made of a filmy, almost vaporous, cloudlike substance. I can see his spirit leaving his body." It seemed to depart from the base of the neck, just where the neck meets the shoulders. His back was to me.

It was only after the full length of his body had departed in spirit form that a small trail of the same substance seemed to be left behind, now seeming attached to, somehow, or flowing out of, his head. It was shaped something like a column, fairly substantial in width but not so wide as Jim's spirit itself. The column seemed flexible, almost as though it were floating freely in the air; yet it was attached both to the body and the spirit.

"It's so strange," I told Scott, "I want to describe this exactly as I'm seeing it. The spirit is moving up through the crevice between the two rocks—up toward the top of the canyon. As it goes up I can recognize it as Jim and I can tell he is smiling, but the form has no features. It is about Jim's height, and it is more or less the shape of the exterior outline of a body, but it has no arms or legs that are distinguishable, and no eyes, nose, or mouth. Yet I can tell he is smiling. And I get such a sense of peace." The tears were a mixture of relief and sadness—and a growing feeling of joy.

56

"It's taking him so long to reach the top of the canyon," I told Scott, "it must be a very long way up to the top. He must be far down the sides of the cliff wall." We waited in silence.

The long white column continued to stretch out along the crevice, still attached to the body. It seemed less substantial now, but it was still definitely there. . . .

"Now he's beginning to go up in the air," I went on. "As he rises up above the canyon, the column is beginning to dissolve from the top. It is drifting away—apart, almost like a cloud when it is blown into wisps by the wind and vanishes in the sky. And his spirit keeps going up."

I had a growing sense of joy to add to the peace I had felt from the beginning. Then suddenly I saw—above Jim—a huge crowd of people waiting.

"My God, Scott, there are *so many people* waiting for him. Hundreds of people—just like a cloud. They are more or less the same height, since they are about the height of human beings; and since they are standing in a big crowd and are suspended in the air, they actually look like a cloud. The sky seems to be dark, but nevertheless the feeling I get is that of a light, billowy cloud against a bright blue sky. . . .

"Now Jim is approaching the crowd. He's moving very slowly. He is so happy, Scott, and so much at peace. It's just beautiful. . . ."

Jim moved on into the midst of the crowd, and then: "They are closing in around him now," I told Scott. "They're gone." The crowd enclosed Jim, and when I could see him no more, they all disappeared.

For the first time I opened my eyes.

"Oh, Scott," I said, "how beautiful! So much joy! Nothing but joy and victory. Jim was so *happy* and so much at peace. What a *beautiful*, beautiful thing."*

I feel certain that the data dramatized or projected visually by my Higher Self in that vision were received on Friday,

---

* From *Search*, copyright © 1969, 1970 by Diane Kennedy Pike. Reprinted by permission of Doubleday & Company, Inc.

but it would appear that until I knew Jim would be found—either dead or alive—my Little Self was not ready to receive these facts and consciously assimilate them. All of us have an internal, protective regulator that governs how much we will have to cope with in the light of full consciousness at any given time. This appears to be a function of our inner wisdom (Higher Self), which *knows* what we (Little Self and body) can handle and what we can't at any given time. It does not release into consciousness other facts, though data are stored in the mind's memory bank to be drawn on later. No amount of probing or prodding can force us to remember what our Little Self and physical systems are not ready to assimilate at a given time. Drugs, it would appear, sometimes chemically trigger physiological memory tapes, playing them "ready or not," often causing "bad trips." But without such externally induced stimulation, our Higher Selves regulate and determine when such memories can be released into consciousness harmoniously and without ill effect.

"Seeing clearly" with the inner eye, or third eye, is sometimes called clairvoyance and sometimes a vision. The term "hallucination" is misleading because it implies that what is seen does not "really" exist. The point is that though what is seen is *not* perceived by the one labeling it a hallucination, it is most certainly real to the perceiver.*

* Many persons whose loved ones have died have reported having experiences of clairvoyance or visions around the time of the death even though they do not ordinarily have such extrasensory experiences. It would appear that the extraordinary openness of the bereaved one to the one who has just made the transition of death, and the energy released in the process of dying itself, account for the unusual number of phenomenal experiences surrounding death. (See, for example, *Deathbed Observations by Physicians and Nurses,* by Karlis Osis, Parapsychological Monographs #3 [1961], Parapsychology Foundation, Inc., 29 West 75th St., New York, N.Y.)

At the time I wrote *Search,* and until the time of this present reflection, I have often said I found it remarkable that my Higher Self was able to project images that could be seen by my *physical eyes* during such a vision. It is clear to me now that my amazement was due to a confusion. I was *not* seeing the

Little-Self Feelings of Higher-Self Perceptions
The principal impact of the vision of Jim's death was to let me know, consciously, not only that Jim's body was already dead but that for him the experience of leaving his body behind had been filled with tremendous joy and peace and a fan-

---

vision with my physical eyes but rather with my inner (third) eye. This is obvious to me now for the following reasons:

1) I could see the vision with my physical eyes either open *or* closed.

2) What I saw as background, and in the periphery, with my physical eyes, I perceived in color. What I was *focused* on, with my attention, was in black and white (perhaps a sign of a third eye only beginning its development or unfolding).

3) Changing my physical location did not interrupt the vision. The vision was a response to my consciousness—or attention, focus, and awareness —not to my location.

4) What I saw in the vision (with my inner eye) was not of the same dimensions as what I saw with my physical eyes. That is to say, the vision was not "life size." It was more like watching a movie. It was not flat, however, but at least 3-D.

The importance of the above observations lies in the realm of a discipline I have chosen for myself. Beginning with my series of breakthroughs to cosmic consciousness in 1965, I decided to report any extraordinary, or extrasensory experiences—those entered into through altered states of consciousness—*exactly* as they happened, leaving explanations and interpretations for later periods of reflection on what actually happened.

As I began here to write about that vision, of which I have written and talked innumerable times since I saw it, I suddenly *understood* that I did not see it with my physical eyes. For four years, I thought I did. But the way I *reported* it was that I saw it with my *eyes open*—a fact I now see as irrelevant, since I also saw it with my eyes closed. Reporting what *actually* happened freed me to come to a new understanding of it and about it in this moment and no doubt will enable me to come to further insights in the future.

This is for me further confirmation of my decision not to restrict my response to new experiences by imposing on them the limited interpretations or understandings I happen to have in any given moment. The experiences stand on their own merit. If I receive them exactly as they are, they enable me to expand my comprehension of my potential as a human being. Interpretations are only overlays I place on my experiences, limiting and sometimes clouding over the potential impact of an experience on my deeper understanding.

tastic sense of victory over death. Thus my Little Self could feel good about Jim and be glad for him, while still being protected by the effects of shock from feeling the full impact of his death on her own life. For weeks, Little Self was able to carry a message to Jim's loved ones, friends, and acquaintances: It's nothing but joy and victory for Jim. Nothing but joy and victory.

This message gave Little Self something to focus on as I went through a series of experiences which might have caused further trauma. But Little Self was being protected by shock —a Higher-Self form of insulation and protection—and was given Higher-Self–induced perceptions and feelings to be with during that difficult time, and this was an enormous blessing. Little Self was able to say "yes" to all I experienced and thus to receive it all in gratitude and joy. Had she responded with resistance and denial—had she said "no" to life as it was coming to her in those moments—she would undoubtedly have experienced still more pain and perhaps even horror. Here I was living out another important principle of higher consciousness perception: what we might ordinarily label *problems* are actually *opportunities* when we open ourselves to the learning and growth available to us in and through them.

For instance, when the police called on me to identify Jim's body, Little Self, because of the vision, felt that Jim was no longer in the body and therefore could let Higher Self be in charge. As a result, the experience of viewing an already decaying corpse was a deeply moving spiritual experience.

The chief of police prepared me for the shock by explaining that the desert is very harsh and bodies decay very rapidly there. He said that the process of dehydration caused the body to swell to almost twice its normal size and to turn black, and that the tissues break down rapidly so that in only a few hours the body is already in a state of advanced decay.

I was glad for that information because I had never seen a body in a state of natural disintegration. My previous experiences had all been in viewing bodies preserved by embalming, lying in caskets, and looking very "normal." People commented, "Doesn't he [or she] look natural?" by which they meant that the body looked as though the person were still alive in it.

With Jim's death, I had the privilege of experiencing what is *actually* natural: in what we call the death of the body there is a clear demonstration of the ongoing nature of life, for death is not in any regard a static state. Once the body dies to the form of life we call "living," it is immediately swept up into a process of transformation. The form is changed so that it may become, or be used by, *other* manifestations of life.

I could still recognize the body as Jim's, though it was enormously bloated and black all over. The head was so swollen that the ears, neck, hair, and nose were almost entirely absorbed into one large mass. The eyeballs had been entirely consumed, leaving only swollen sockets, and the open mouth also seemed only a cavity lined with swollen flesh. His shirt had burst open with the pressure of the swelling, and the sleeves pinched his arms. His pant legs were pulled up by the swelling, leaving bulges around the ankles, where his socks and shoes still held the oversized feet. When I asked to see his left arm, which was tucked under the body, I was surprised to see that it hung absolutely limp. I had not known until then that rigor mortis lasts only a few hours even under normal circumstances, and that when putrefaction (the decay of the tissues) begins, the whole body goes limp.

Jim's wedding ring was still on his third finger, but it had sunk into the flesh down to the bone. Maggots crawled on, around, and under it, busily doing their work of transformation. They had already consumed a large part of the flesh of the fingers, leaving white flesh exposed, flecked with the pink remains of blood.

I looked with wonder. It was my husband's body—and yet it was so clearly *not* his body anymore. Once Jim had ceased to function in and through his body, it began to be altered so it could serve other life forms as it had previously served Jim. All was progressing according to the natural order: ashes to ashes and dust to dust.

I saw nothing but beauty in that body, for it was life itself moving on, changing, growing. There was no "cessation" of life in death; there was rather a new form emerging for life's expression—a process not unlike birth in that regard. A decaying corpse was not a horrible or ugly sight. It was, rather, a vivid and wonderful expression of the miracle of life.

At no time since then has the memory of that day, and Jim's decayed body, been in any way painful or nightmarish to Little Self. It therefore seems clear to me that when my Little Self is in harmony with my Higher Self and functions in response to Higher-Self perceptions, my feelings are free-flowing and life-affirming and in no way cause pain. This was an important lesson for me to learn, and it has served as a guideline for me during the years since then as I have sought to bring my Little Self into complete integration with my Higher Self.

On that Sunday—the day I identified Jim's body—Higher Self put a seal on the images of Jim stored in my memory bank. This was a protection for Little Self, as I came to appreciate later, but for weeks Little Self felt terrible that she had so soon forgotten what Jim looked like. I kept his pictures everywhere so that Little Self could be reminded. Little Self felt she had "forgotten"; Higher Self would have said she was being protected from remembering.

Arranging for the Burial

I was glad Jim and I had talked rather extensively about funerals and burials before I had to make decisions about his. I knew that he had preferred simplicity of arrangements and cremation of the remains.

Once I had seen Jim's body already well into its process of becoming one with the land onto which it had fallen, I felt deeply that the body should remain there in Israel. To remove it would have seemed a gross interruption of the natural-order process.

I at once inquired about cremation, only to learn that it was forbidden by law in the state of Israel. Then I asked about burial there. I learned there were only three Protestant burial sites in the whole country—one in Galilee, one near Bethlehem, and one in Jaffa. The body had already been taken to the Forensic Institute in Tel Aviv for the autopsy, so I decided that we would look at the cemetery in nearby Jaffa and, if it was acceptable, bury the body there.

Meanwhile, I called home to consult with Jim's mother and his three children, to see if they agreed that the body should be buried in Israel. To have flown it home would have cost an exorbitant amount of money (fifteen hundred dollars just for the airfare, if I remember correctly), and because of the advanced state of putrefaction, no one in the States could have viewed the body in any case. Once it had been sealed into a coffin it could not, for health reasons, have been reopened. For that reason, to transport the body to California seemed an enormous waste. And in addition, I felt it "belonged" in Israel. I was relieved, then, when Jim's mother and children agreed to Israel as the burial place.

Immediately after receiving the autopsy report early Monday morning (just one week after Jim and I had left to take that fateful drive into the wilderness), my brother and I went by taxi to the American Embassy in Tel Aviv, where, I had been told, I needed to make arrangements for the burial. I had to sign some official documents authorizing burial arrangements for an American citizen in a foreign country. Then the Embassy gave me the phone number of the priest in charge of the Protestant cemetery in neighboring Jaffa.

Father Knight turned out to be an Episcopalian, and we learned that the Episcopal Church had custody over the Protestant cemetery. Somehow that made us feel good about the

63

site even before we saw it. We went right over to the church in Jaffa, and Father Knight then took us to see the cemetery itself. It is a small burial ground, tucked alongside a Roman Catholic cemetery that lies to the north and bordering on the Mediterranean Sea to the west. Pine trees shade the older part of the cemetery, and we walked in stillness down the dusty path to the open area nearest the water, where burial plots were available. There one lonely tree stood, giving some shade in the heat of the day. Immediately I said, "That is perfect."

The week's search for Jim had been interminably long. Suddenly all I wanted was to have it all over with so that I could go home. With me were my brother Scott and John and Ellen Downing, friends and colleagues from California who had been flown in through the generosity of a friend who felt they should be with me. John was also an Episcopal priest, and he had moved to Santa Barbara to work with Jim and me in our Foundation for Religious Transition.

Scott, Ellen, and John agreed with me that the site was lovely. I asked Henry Knight to make arrangements with the custodian to dig the grave that very afternoon, offering to pay him extra for working in the heat of the midday sun. Then the five of us returned to the church, where we made the rest of the arrangements for the committal.

I called the Forensic Institute and asked if I could bury the body in the aluminum box they had used to transport it from Bethlehem to Tel Aviv. They said that I could. They also agreed to deliver the body to the cemetery at five o'clock that afternoon. Then Father Knight took us all downtown so I could find a simple cotton dress to wear for the service. Scott found and purchased a golden wool rug to drape over the casket. Later, John and I planned the simple service.

Committing the Body to the Earth

Around 4:30 P.M. two gentlemen called for us in a limousine sent by the American Embassy. As we drove toward the

64

cemetery, I realized we would be late in arriving for the appointed 5 P.M. hour. Instantly I recalled one of Jim's favorite sayings. He was often late for speaking engagements, and as we would be making our way there he would say, "Don't worry; they can't start the funeral without the corpse." Now we were about to arrive late for his own funeral. Out loud I said to Scott and the Downings, "It looks like we'll be late, but as Jim always used to say, 'They can't start the funeral without the corpse.'"

We all burst into laughter—an incredible relief after the almost inconceivable tension and strain of the last week. As laughter subsided, I recalled two other "funeral" jokes Jim used to tell. Somehow they had never seemed more relevant, so I told them to Scott and the Downings. After each, the four of us again laughed heartily, enjoying the humor of the jokes told in precisely the right setting.

When we grew silent once more, I addressed the two gentlemen in front. "I hope you can understand," I said rather feebly. "My husband always had a wonderful sense of humor." It had occurred to me that they might think our laughter inappropriate. But then as now I felt that nothing could be a finer tribute to our beloved Jim than to respond to his death as we did to his life—with our whole selves, with laughter *and* tears, joy *and* sorrow. For life was moving on *in us* as well as in Jim.

The committal service was simple and beautiful. As I tossed the first handsful of dirt on the lowered box, I felt that only one thing would have been more appropriate, and that would have been if the health laws had permitted putting the body directly in the ground with no box at all so that the natural processes could have continued entirely uninterrupted. But we had done it as simply as possible, and I felt that Jim would be at peace about it, as were we.

It had been a deep privilege to live through the entire cycle of death, with no well-intentioned interference by funeral directors or others who might have wanted to "spare" me some of that in-depth life experience. I treasured the experience because it was grounded in reality. I had seen the body in its "decay." The body had been placed in the ground with as little interference as possible in the natural-order process of transformation. My brother Scott and friend John had helped lower it into the grave. I had begun the process of covering it with earth with my own bare hands. I had been one with Jim in death as in life, and I vowed that never again would I consciously be a party to "hiding" the wonder and beauty of death from anyone—as is so often done in our society.

The inscription later put on the gravestone accurately reflects my Higher-Self perception of death of the physical body as well as the feelings I had in my Little Self on the day of that burial service: "We have this treasure in earthen vessels, to show that the transcendent power belongs to God and not to us" (II Cor. 4:7) "And Life Is Victorious!" (Mandaean Book of Prayer).

3

SHOCK

*Higher Self's Protection
of Little Self*

THERE ARE SOME EXPERIENCES in life which seem to stretch
out in length to match all the rest of it put together. That
week in Israel and my first week at home were like that. There
doesn't seem to be any way to recapture in words the intensity
of those days, and it was the intensity that made them seem
lifelong.

After the burial service in Jaffa, we were driven back to
our hotel in Jerusalem so that we could pack. I don't remember now how it happened, but sometime during that long
Monday I had requested that Peggy Barnhart, the woman
from the American Consulate in Jerusalem who had been so
very helpful to me, get us four reservations to California for
the next day. We were to leave on an early plane out of Tel
Aviv—Scott and I with first-class reservations, and Ellen and
John on standby.

As the four of us entered the hotel, I noticed a dress shop
still open. In the window stood a manikin wearing a vibrant
green wool dress and coat. I stopped to look. "Jim had said he
wanted to buy me a green wool dress here in Israel," I told
Scott. "That's exactly the color of green."

"Do you want to try it on?" Scott asked.

"Perhaps we could just ask what size they have it in," I said. As I went through the door I felt my weariness—yet there was a desire to link up Jim's and my past with our new present. It's hard to describe the feeling, but it was as though by buying the dress Jim had wanted to get me, I could move on in the rhythm of our life together, not noticing quite so dramatically all the plans that his sudden death had left unfulfilled.

I asked the saleslady about the dress in the window. "It's our last one like that," she replied.

"What size is it?" I inquired.

"Sixteen," she said matter-of-factly.

"Another part of the perfect pattern," I commented to Scott and the Downings. "May I try it on?" I asked the saleslady.

The dress was a perfect fit, and with my last traveler's checks, I paid her for it, not really caring what it cost. It was Jim's gift to me. I would wear it to the Requiem Mass: rich green, the color that symbolizes new life.

There is something almost superhuman about being in shock. In spite of my exhaustion, I kept functioning. I took care of the details of checking out at the desk. There were enormous telephone bills and many extra room charges. Not until the moment I stood before the desk to pay the bill had I thought about the costs. "May I put this on a credit card?" I asked.

The cashier consulted the manager. It was not their custom to charge such a large bill, but under the circumstances . . .

I gratefully received all the courtesies extended to me by the hotel management and staff, the American Consulate, the Israeli police and army, our friends in Israel. Never once did I stop the flow with feelings of unworthiness or false strength. I was in great need, and I received most gratefully all that was given to me. *Providing people with the opportunity to give* is another of those principles for higher-consciousness living which I later came to recognize as having enabled me to function in harmony during that time of crisis.

I was up late, packing and getting ready to leave. Early the next morning a bellboy came to get my bags. I was in tears. He said, "Are you all right, madam?"

"Yes; it's just very hard to leave here without my husband," I wept.

"Life is like that," the young Arab said, looking upon me in compassion. "Where is my father? Where is my mother?" he asked, shrugging his shoulders. "I do not know. Life is like that."

In times of sorrow and grief there is a strange but beautiful bond that ties together all those who have known bereavement. Even strangers are kinsfolk in those moments, for they know and understand us better, often, than those closest to us who have never gone through a similar separation and loss.

Plans for the Requiem

I had called home on Sunday with my requests that a Requiem Mass be arranged at Grace Cathedral in San Francisco. I asked two of Jim's close friends, the Reverend Robert E. Hoggard and the Reverend Darby Betts, to take charge of planning it, and made only a few suggestions and requests of my own.

On Monday night Bob Hoggard had called. He told me how the plans were progressing. One of Jim's friends whom I had asked to concelebrate the Mass would be out of the state, he reported. And what should we do about Kim?

Kim Myers was the bishop of the diocese, and it was only appropriate, in terms of protocol, that he officiate at the Mass. Yet our last official interchange with Kim had been the unhappy one having to do with his disapproval of Jim's and my marriage. Bishop Myers had been the direct catalyst for our leaving the Church, through his personal request that Jim no longer be invited to serve as a priest in his diocese or elsewhere in the country. I knew Jim had not held that against Kim. He had, in fact, talked with Kim by telephone not long before we left the country, saying he hoped they could soon get together and talk about those unfortunate events so that they would not stand between them. I knew if Jim were in my shoes, he would invite Bishop Myers to be the principal celebrant at the Mass, but I wasn't sure I could or would. "Let me think about it, Bob, and I'll tell you my decision when I get home," I said.

I spent the entire twenty-hour plane trip home purging myself of my resentments of Kim for what he had done to Jim. I knew *Jim* had held no resentments. He never had. He had been quick not only to forgive but also to forget any injuries done him. But now that Jim was gone, I suddenly felt intense resentment on his behalf. It was as though, because he was no longer here to fight his own, I felt I had to take on some battles for him.

I wrestled with myself, wanting to do what Jim would have done, yet choosing not to do anything that would violate my own inner feelings. Either I had to be able to completely forgive Kim Myers for what he had done, or I would not invite him to take part in the Requiem Mass.

The trip was long enough for me to resolve my feelings. I let go of resentment and let love flood in. I was able to *receive* Kim *as beautiful exactly where he was*—another key to higher consciousness living. I forgave Kim for what he had done and determined that he should be the principal celebrant at the Mass.

Again, Higher Self was in charge, but not without keen sensitivity to the deep feelings of Little Self. It was important to me that I act as one harmonious whole and that there not be pockets of unfinished emotional business left festering anywhere in my being.

Not Alone in my Grief

My parents had requested that the press not be at the airport when we arrived. I was grateful for that. The strain had been enormous during the week in Israel, and daily interviews by the press had added to that strain. My whole family was there waiting for us as Scott and I came out of customs. I felt almost numb, not knowing how I continued to move.

I remember little of our conversation as we drove to my parents' home in San Jose. I was still riding on that joy energy that the vision had released in me yet I was aware of the enormous exhaustion of my physical body.

We talked until almost two that morning, pouring out our stories of what it had been like in Israel and what it had been like in San Jose. Until that time, I had not turned my attention to what others must be going through. Now I began to grasp the magnitude of the involvement of others in "my" grief.

I remember with a special sense of poignancy my father's telling of his decision to send Scott to Israel as the family's representative. "I knew I would be of no help to you," he said softly. "I had never been out of the country; I didn't know Israel. I knew I would only be a burden to you as you would have to watch after me. Scott had been to Israel with you. He knew you and Jim better than any of the rest of us. He was the logical one to send. And yet, I said to myself"—he shook his head slowly, left and right. Tears were now streaming down his face—"what kind of a father am I that I would send my youngest son to do what I know I cannot do myself? If anything had happened to him . . ."

He did not finish the sentence, but he didn't need to. Suddenly I realized that the trauma, the tension, the intensity, and the grief were not entirely my own.

Shock and My Body

My body began to come out of its state of shock first. It had been only partially numbed by Higher Self—numbed so that it felt no pain, but not so that it could not function fully and efficiently.

I had never so clearly distinguished, before going through grief, the difference between *physical* pain, and *emotional* pain that manifests physically. During the weeks and months I was grieving, I began to see clearly the difference between the two through my own experience of them, and my awareness of that difference has been of great help to me since then.

It was on September 10, almost nine full days after I made my journey through the wilderness, that I began to feel aches and pains. I had taxed my body to its limits and beyond during my fourteen-hour trek through the wilderness, causing great strain and inflicting multiple injuries upon my physical being. Now the "numbness" began to wear off.

My muscles began to ache terrifically and eventually to get stiff—as would have been natural the day after such a strenuous "hike" under normal circumstances. I felt pain in my scratches, punctures, and bruises, and my badly sprained ankle began to ache for the first time. Even the swelling (which had not begun until after I got help for Jim and the police began the search) had not caused stiffness or pain until then.

My body had been—and remained—very tense, the physical reflection of the fact that I was holding in almost all of my Little Self feelings. Partly because of that physical tension related to the emotional shock I was still in, and partly because I was so filled with Higher Self energy, I was sleeping very little at night. My pattern for the six days of the search and the first few days after I returned to the States was to sleep two hours, awaken, sleep two more hours, and wake up again.

After my return to California, I stayed with my parents in

San Jose for about ten days. I noticed by the third day at home that my insomnia made it impossible for Mother and Dad to sleep too. That they mirrored for me in their own physical bodies what was actually going on in my own was a great gift to me, for then I could make a new choice. On September 11, for the first time since the day I returned from the desert and was hysterical, I took two aspirin and a sleeping pill in an attempt to shock myself in reverse, so to speak, into going to sleep. Since I so seldom take medication of any kind, it worked. That night I slept five hours uninterrupted, and I knew the pattern had been broken. I was also relieved to find that my parents were now able to sleep, too.

Jim and the Requiem Mass

The Requiem Mass and Memorial Service was held at noon on Friday, September 12, 1969, at Grace Cathedral in San Francisco. I dressed in my verdant wool Israeli dress and coat, the weather having obliged by being cool and overcast that day, and felt wrapped in Jim's love as we drove from San Jose to the city.

Bob Hoggard had suggested that Jim's mother and aunt, my family and I go to a nearby mortuary so we could be driven to the Cathedral in limousines. Immediately my Little Self had balked, wanting nothing to do with what she felt would be the moroseness of the funereal atmosphere. But Bob prevailed, insisting it would simplify parking and our entering the Cathedral. I had finally acquiesced, asserting I would not go in the place but would wait in the parking lot.

When the day came, however, I agreed to wait in the entrance hall until it was time for us to go. Someone went to get sandwiches for us, and I was nervous and restless. But the mortuary was surprisingly pleasant, friendly, and light-filled. I remember commenting several times about the pleasing environment. I was glad I had not clung to *expectations* based on imagination rather than actual experience, but had instead

73

proceeded with *abundant expectancy* and openness to the new.

At five minutes to the hour, we were delivered at the Cathedral's back door by the limousines. Bob Hoggard was waiting at the door for us, and he took me by the arm to lead me to my seat. As we entered the Cathedral proper I was immediately struck by the magnificent radiance of the stained-glass windows all around the clerestory of the Cathedral. The sun was not yet shining through the clouds, but the *Light* was shining, and it was brilliant. I had never seen the windows shine like that. Immediately I felt that Jim's presence was responsible for the glow, and Little Self soared again on Higher-Self joy.

Jim, while Bishop of California, had been largely responsible for the completion of the construction of Grace Cathedral, and he loved it with a pride in beauty as he loved little else. The windows glowed for/with/by him through the entire service, and as the Mass was about to end, the sun broke through the clouds and also shone through the windows above the altar. But the other Light was no dimmer. Many others in attendance reported to me later that they also had seen the radiance in the windows.

Perhaps the highlight of the service for me was the opportunity I had to greet people as they came forward to receive communion. I was seated on the aisle in the front pew on the left. As people passed by, I spontaneously reached out to them, or they to me, and we embraced. Over and over again I was able to deliver the message: "It's nothing but joy and victory for Jim. Nothing but joy and victory." And with each sharing, my own joy increased. It was a grace-filled experience. I felt infused with the love, peace, and joy of God, and surrounded and bathed in Jim's presence at the same time.

A *Little-Self Withdrawal*

It was the day after the Requiem Mass that I had my first letdown. Esther had been Jim's wife for twenty-five years and

74

is the mother of his four children. She and I had met in person only once and had talked on the telephone the day before the Requiem only in order to determine seating arrangements at the Cathedral. Esther had wanted to avoid embarrassment. I had felt totally at ease with the prospect of her presence there.

Jim and Esther had three surviving children. Christopher is the youngest, and I knew him quite well, for he had spent a considerable amount of time with Jim and me in Santa Barbara, even living with us for a time.

Constance Ann is the middle child (since Jim, Jr.'s, death). She had traveled with Jim, my brother Scott, and me to the Middle East in 1968 and had also spent time in Santa Barbara with us, so, again, I felt I knew Connie quite well.

Catherine Hope is the oldest. She had married just a year after I met Jim, and though the time we had spent with Cathy and Chuck had been less extensive than with the other two children, we had been able to share deeply and maturely with them, and I felt that a warm and open relationship had been established between us.

On the day after the Requiem, Esther and I were discussing plans for the children to come to San Jose to see me. I wanted to share with them in detail, and in person, what had happened to Jim and me in the desert, and I was especially eager to share the vision with them. I felt it would be a comfort to them as it had been to me. I offered to share it with Esther, too, if she would like.

During the time Jim was alive, I had felt nothing but understanding and caring about and for Esther. I used to spend much time and energy helping Jim to absorb and let go of the deep pain he suffered nearly every time he talked with Esther or heard from her, so I was familiar with many of their relational patterns. But my Little Self had never gotten involved in them and harbored no negative feelings toward Esther at all.

That Saturday evening, September 13, Esther made several comments that my Little Self (who was being totally open to everyone, including Esther, and thus was very vulnerable) experienced as sharp knife-thrusts into her heart center. She absorbed the unexpected pain in silence and terminated the conversation quickly. Then she stood in stunned silence in the kitchen.

Higher Self was still there, observing, but Little Self had gone "dead" inside. She had received Esther's comments the way *Jim* would have received them, had suffered the deep pain *he* would have suffered, and then had no other energy with which to respond to the hurt. She gave up.

From my Higher-Self vantage point I watched the drama that ensued. I could not reach my Little Self. She had closed off her energy channels as a protective device against further hurt and thus was unable to respond even to love. She was no longer *providing people with the opportunity to give* to her. I knew that family members would try to reach her. I didn't know if they would be able to. She was in something similar to a catatonic state.

My mother spoke first. "What happened, Diane?" she asked. My Little Self heard the question but did not respond. I (Higher Self) realized that without Little-Self energy I could not speak even though I could think thoughts. I knew that my family would worry about me, but Higher Self could not reach them with reassurance.

My Little Self stood in stunned silence. Mother asked what Esther had said. Again no response. Then Jim's aunt Ethyl came to put her hands on my shoulders. She said a lot of words that were true and would ordinarily have been a comfort, but Little Self did not respond. Ethyl went to her room in distress.

Then Jim's mother tried. Pearl put her arms around me lovingly. She spoke to me of Jim, of Esther, of how she loved me, of how Jim loved me, of how I should not take what others said to heart. She spoke truths, too, and many deeply loving and caring words. But Little Self did not muster any response—not even a return embrace. Pearl turned to Mother in obvious pain and despair. "I'll leave you with her. She probably wants to be with her own mother," she said. Pearl went quietly off to her room.

Mother began to talk to me again. I knew of her love and her genuine concern. I wished there were a way to help her help my Little Self. But I was dumb without Little Self's energy, and she was lifeless within me.

I don't know how long Mother talked to me, speaking wise words, loving words, comforting words. Finally my father arrived home. It was now near 10 P.M. He asked what was wrong. Mother told him as much as she knew.

Crackers and Milk

Dad took charge of his little girl. He talked a bit. Then he said, "Don't you want to go to bed now?" Little Self shook her head. "Why don't you sleep with your mother tonight? You'll feel better not being alone." Little Self shook her head again. "Well, at least come in and rest for a while. You'll feel better," he said reassuringly. Little Self acquiesced.

As I stretched out—tense, but lying down—Dad stood at the door. It was evident he was looking for something to say that might be helpful. Then he reached back into his own experiences with death and shared as he had never before shared his thoughts about the feelings he had had at his mother's death when he was twelve, and his reactions to things others said to him then, as well as about other death-experiences he had gone through. He shared the wisdom he had gained about not listening to and taking into oneself the opinions of others.

My Higher Self saw how deeply moving his sharing was, and Little Self heard every word. Dad had reached her. Something of life was beginning to stir in her again. But she did not speak.

Then—as though a stroke of genius had touched him—my

father said, "How would you like to have a bowl of crackers and milk?"

In our family, Dad and Mother had often "fixed" our hurts and ills when we were children by preparing us a bowl of crackers and milk, with sugar. I can remember many an occasion when I was a little girl and the blackest of skies cleared for me as I finished off such a "remedy."

My Little Self stirred, smiled weakly, and said, "That sounds good."

"Here," Dad said, tossing me a robe. Then he fairly bounded into the kitchen, where he threw open the cupboard and got out a bowl. Mother came in from the dining room as I slowly shuffled in. "What's going on?" she asked, obviously surprised.

"I'm fixing Diane some crackers and milk," Dad said with all the pride and joy of a father who has just scored again with his unfailing home remedy for ills. I sat down. He served me a generous bowl with plenty of sugar. I ate it up and asked for a second.

Mother and Dad were chattering quietly, visibly relieved to see me responding again. My brother Scott came in from an evening out. As he entered the kitchen, he stopped to take in the scene: it's nearly midnight; Mother is seated at the table; Dad is pacing the floor; Diane, in her robe, is eating crackers and milk.

"It must have been a *heavy* evening," he said, speaking out of the knowledge of one who knows from experience that "crackers and milk + sugar = healed hurts and copious parental love and caring."

That was the first of several occasions during my grief in which I knew the enormous blessing of having living parents who could minister to my Little Self and their little girl when she was in deep pain. Nothing has touched me more deeply than those precious moments.

This was also the first time I was consciously aware that

sometimes the only way I am able to get reconnected with my own energy flow is to allow someone else to plug into me and complete the circuit for me. Once the current is flowing again, I am back in touch with myself.

To reach the Little Self through another person is an alternative that the Higher Self can choose when the more direct approach does not work. Such is not an indication of weakness, as I once thought, but rather a perceiving and receiving of the wholeness of the universe, and a realization that there is no separation between me and another, nor between us and the All. To establish contact with another is to be in contact with myself and the One, or God, all at once. When I *provide others with the opportunity to give* to me, I open myself to the Love Force of the universe and once again have something to give myself.

The Return to Our House

About six days later, my mother, Scott, and I drove down to Santa Barbara to Jim's and my home. I wanted to get back. It seemed important to me that life move on.

Little Self felt ready to face the return to Santa Barbara, but as we were driving up into the hills where our house was located, panic began to overtake her. My mind imagined we would get there and the house would be burned to the ground. Little Self responded in fear, for then, she felt, she would *really* have nothing. That was the beginning of a fantasy that persisted for months. Every time I would be away for a period of time and would be on my way back home, an image of the house burned to the ground would surface and cause waves of nausea and panic to pass through Little Self.

This makes me realize how much a house can symbolize for a grief-stricken Little Self. It is an external reminder that her world is not entirely destroyed, that she has one last bastion of security: her home.

There was a strange irony in that Little Self reaction for

79

me. Jim and I had not thought of our house as the place where our roots were, for we knew our roots, and our security, were internal and portable. But obviously the feelings of a deeply wounded Little Self were quite different. During grief, my house—our home—was a comfort and a security for me, and had I not been able to remain in it, my pain would surely have been more difficult to cope with.

When we entered the house that day, I was overwhelmed with a tremendous awareness of an energy void. This void was due to the absence of Jim's physical, emotional, and mental energies. I sensed his presence on a Higher Self plane, but his absence on those other three planes—and especially physically and emotionally—was dramatic.

Jim was a dynamo of energy. He filled any room he entered—even large halls or gymnasiums—with a vitality that had the capacity to make everyone feel more alive. In our house he had filled each room with movement, purposeful interchange, and a sense of excitement and life just by *being*. Now that tremendous energy output/input was gone from this physical plane. Throughout my body and in the pit of my stomach where the solar plexus—the center of all emotions—is located, I felt the void he had left.

I wandered about, looking at things. Then another giant wave of realization swept over Little Self—that only *things* were left for me. The paradox was incredibly painful. Jim and I had cared so little for objects, possessions. Now *he* was gone (Little Self perception again) and I was left with *them*. Little Self felt resentful of them for taking Jim's place.

A great sense of burden came over me. It was as though the world had been dumped on my shoulders at a time when three fourths of my energy was gone. "I'm twice the person I was before I met Jim," I told Mother and Scott, "but three fourths of me is gone."

Little Self felt unable to cope with that giant world on her shoulders, but she *could* talk about it. Mother sat beside me on the couch with her arm around me, and Scott sat across from me in a chair as I reported to them all I was feeling. I wept long and hard, and then I felt somewhat relieved.

In Place of Decision

Mother gave me many gifts of love during the time she stayed with me, but perhaps the greatest gift she gave me was to offer to pack Jim's clothes away so I would not have to think about them. She made this offer on my first day at home when I was still feeling overwhelmed. Little Self did not know what she wanted, but she trusted Mother's judgment that it would be hard for me to do anything with the clothes for some time, and that by her packing them for me, and hanging his suits in the closet in the garage, I could wait until I felt like it to make decisions about disposing of them.

Just how wise Mother was I realized as the days wore on, for it was well over a year before I was able to touch even his shaving things, which she had neglected to take away. Each time I would look at them, Little Self would go weak inside and say, *I just can't.* Little Self was unwilling to finalize the physical absence of Jim. Higher Self knew they had to go eventually, but Higher Self also had the wisdom never to wrench Little Self away from anything before she felt the strength to cope with it. Finally, Jim's and my close friend Bob Hoggard came to visit one day, and my Little Self was able to entrust Jim's shaving kit to him, relieved to have it gone at last and satisfied to have a trusted friend dispose of, or use, it.

On my second day at home, at my request, a meeting of the Board of Directors of the Foundation for Religious Transition was held. Jim and I had organized the Foundation in order that we, and others, might minister to the needs of priests, ministers, and other church professionals who were leaving their employment in the institutional church and beginning new lives in the secular world.

The Foundation was one thing that I felt I just couldn't

carry. It was the burden Little Self felt would break her back, and it was the opportunity Higher Self saw should either be met with full energy or turned away. I expressed all of this to the Board and asked that they either put someone else in charge or close the Foundation.

They acted as they felt best, changing the name to The Bishop Pike Foundation and appointing John Downing as Executive Director. Their plan was to expand the Foundation in the direction of, and along the lines of, that which Jim and I had originally envisioned.

The plans did not work out as the Board had hoped, and though I tried to stay out from under it, the financial burden was mine, and with it much of the supervisory responsibility. After a few months I let all but one of the secretaries go and put activities and planning on a back burner until I could finish at least the major part of my grief work.

I feel now, in retrospect, that my inclinations were right at that first meeting. We should either have found someone to take over the Foundation completely, including its financing, or we should have closed it. But undoubtedly there were lessons for all of us to learn in proceeding as we did. I did not finally close the Foundation until May of 1972—two and a half years later. It was not until then that I mustered enough Little Self strength to do what Higher Self long before saw needed to be done. Yet there were advantages to having waited, so I am sure nothing that happened was by accident.

Decisions about joint business ventures or projects or plans that have been shared with the deceased loved one are perhaps the most difficult to make during grief. Usually the decisions cannot wait, because the lives and activities and employment of others depend on them. However, so much energy is channeled into the handling of grief itself that there is very little left with which to make such major decisions.

Usually what happens is that the grieving person relies on the "good advice" of friends and relatives, and decisions are made that see everyone through the most difficult time of transition. Then, when the bereaved is stronger, new decisions can be made that are in harmony with what that person wants to do and can do.

It is important, therefore, insofar as is possible, that doors not be permanently closed by early decisions. They are not likely to seem satisfactory to the grieving person when he or she is able to give more energy and attention to the decision-making process, and if the options have been narrowed or restricted, the result can be regret, remorse, resentment, and even bitterness.

In my case, I felt I would have done better to close the Foundation right after Jim's death, and certainly I would have had far more money at my disposal to do whatever *new* things emerged for me if I had not invested so much in a Foundation that eventually had to be closed anyway.

However, I knew that everyone had acted in good faith, as had I. All had exercised their best judgment and had carried on in a way they felt fitting to Jim's memory. I, in turn, had kept on choosing to put more of my (Jim's and my) money into the staffing and promotion—something no one forced me to do but I did of my own free will. That I was not strong enough to insist on what I knew, from inside, to be better for me was in no way their fault *or* mine. So when I finally did muster the strength to say, "That's it. We are closing the Foundation," I did so with freedom and with no resentments or regrets. I was relieved to be free at last from the burden, and I think my friends and co-workers were relieved, as well.

A Glimpse of Suffering

On my fourth day at home in Santa Barbara I had my first graphic flash-memory of Jim. I had been talking with my mother at the dining room table. I got up to go downstairs to the office to do some work with the secretaries. As I was passing through the kitchen door into the hall, I remembered vividly a time when I had met Jim right there by the steps, and we had put our arms around each other and started to walk toward our bedroom.

As the memory came in, it was as though someone had physically socked me in the solar plexus, so strong was the energy impact on my Little Self. I reeled backward, stumbled across the kitchen, and collapsed in tears on a chair at the dining room table.

"What is it?" Mother asked.

It was a long time before Little Self could say what had happened, but as she did, she felt deeply what a blessing it had been *not* to be able to recall memories of Jim. She felt deep gratitude for the memory blackout, and Higher Self must have taken note of the pain that even so fleeting a recall had caused, for I did not then come out of shock. It was apparently not yet time to end that protection.

It was following that incident that Little Self began to "relate" to Jim again, sending him brief little prayer thoughts throughout the day. "I love you, darling," she would say. Or, "Don't worry about me. I want you to give your full attention to what your new situation is." Or, "Thank you, sweetheart, for loving me." I felt that these thought-prayers always met Jim, or connected with his vibrations. Little Self was reassured by them.

Higher Self never once felt a break in relationship or communication with Jim. From the day I identified his body, Higher Self felt an unbroken Oneness with him and an open vibrational line that continues to this day.

In spite of her thought-prayers, Little Self entered into a kind of depression after that memory glimpse. I know now that what I experienced as depression was literally my holding down, or back, the pain-filled emotional energy that Little Self was not yet ready to let surface into consciousness.

I was depressing my Little Self energies, and I chose to let her reconnect with more affirming energies by reaching out not only to Mother and Scott but also to three of my closest friends, Pat Rohrs, Patricia Bradley, and Betsy Koester. Sharing with them enabled Little Self to relax somewhat and take into herself some of the renewing energies sent to her by loving friends and family. Once again, I *provided others with the opportunity to give* to me, and reaped a harvest of love as a result.

Communication with Jim

One of the most common experiences reported by persons who have "lost" loved ones through death is that of communicating with the loved one in one form or another after his death. I had read a great deal about such experiences because of Jim's conviction that he had communicated, with the help of a medium, with his son Jim, Jr., after Jim, Jr.'s, death.* I was not surprised then, as many people are, when I had occasions of sensing Jim's presence. I did, however, record these experiences carefully, for I did not want Little Self's desires and needs to cloud or distort any real "messages" that might come through.

During the time period from September 18 to October 1, I had a number of dream-state experiences in which I was in communication with Jim. They were of several varieties. In some Jim himself appeared. I knew in the dreams that he had died and that he had come back to be with me. In these dreams—while I was still in shock—his return seemed related to preparing me for the *fact* of his death. On September 20, for example, I recorded in my dream log: "It was as if Jim had wanted to show me I *could* get along without him—give me a trial period [meaning the time from his death in Israel until that dream experience] so that when death really came, I would have that assurance. And it was true that things had worked out exceptionally well considering the tremendous loss of Jim."

---

* For Jim, Sr.'s, own account of these experiences, see James A. Pike with Diane Kennedy, *The Other Side,* New York: Doubleday & Co., 1968.

These dreams seemed to be a reassurance to my Little Self that she could handle the *fact* of Jim's death in full consciousness. Until then she had not fully faced his death emotionally.

There were other dreams that had to do specifically with mediumship or communication. On September 18, for example, I had the following dream:

Shortly before 6:30 A.M. I woke up, having had a dream in which Jim and I were with the whole family at some big hotel. It had lots of floors, huge parking lots and there seemed to be some convention going on at which Jim was speaking. I knew Jim was along. We had ridden in the elevator together a couple of times and so forth. But I first recognized him (looking at him) from the side (his right side) because he had a little white patch on the spot on the part of his hair that he used to scratch all the time. Apparently we had come in two cars, and as we were leaving, I asked if I should drive and everyone seemed to agree that I should. But when I got in the car, I was all alone. I first felt very deserted because everyone else had gone in the other car, so I went over and said, "Do I have to ride all that way by myself?" Mother was in the back seat on the right side and she seemed to be paying attention to what I was saying. Dad, who was driving, also seemed to hear me. But Jim was leaning over—he was in the right-hand seat in the front of the car, sitting with Dad—and if he heard, didn't seem concerned. I could see then that he had a whole piece of adhesive tape over the spot on his head where he used to scratch. As I stood waiting for Jim to say something or respond, he sat up and I saw his full face. I started to glance away. Then I thought, why should I be afraid to look into his eyes? I was never afraid before. In fact, it was a joy. So I looked into his eyes.

Immediately I was awake, though I could still hold the image of Jim's face if I wanted. Now I was thinking of what Arthur Ford's book* says about communicating, and I decided to stick with it. I was lying on my back with my head turned slightly to the

* *Nothing So Strange.* New York; Harper & Row, 1958.

86

right. I kept my eyes closed and kept looking into Jim's eyes. I could begin to feel, all at once, a fantastic relaxation begin, first in my legs. Knowing how utterly tense I have been for weeks, I was amazed. It was as though looking into Jim's eyes was draining off all the tension. The feeling crept up my body to the lower back. I was trying to breathe deeply, too, and as the feeling crept into my arms I began to be afraid—not of Jim, but of the experience. "If I go into a hypnotic trance, please wake me up before too long," I asked Jim. I could feel the feeling creep over me—through my chest area to my shoulders. I felt my head position was wrong. It needed to be straight. But I hated to move and anyway I wasn't sure I really wanted to go under. I would rather do it with Scott present so he could eventually wake me up if need be, I thought. I had trouble continuing to look into Jim's eyes because I felt the process continuing as I did. By now my whole body was relaxed and tingling. It felt beautiful. Then I stopped looking so I could move my pillow and straighten my head, and when I did I lost it. But I felt a numbness and when I closed my eyes again I could still sense Jim's presence and felt he was filling my body and draining off tension out of concern for me. I felt very close and loving with Jim and was really grateful for the experience.

I turned over and went back to sleep. Then I had another dream where Kristin [my little niece] dove into a deep well-like pool of water. I watched her go all the way to the bottom and was amazed how deep it was. The water was absolutely clear, and I watched her start to swim back up to the top. I could see she wasn't going to make it. I was going to dive in to save her, but Thyra [my sister-in-law, Kristin's mother] asked what was happening. I explained and then said I didn't even know if I could save Kristin [a symbol for my Little Self, perhaps] because I hadn't dived into the well myself and didn't know if I could turn my big body around in it or not.

When I woke up, the import seemed to be about my diving into the well of mediumship. I remembered the time Jim had gone into trance in an Esalen Institute workshop, and John Heider [psychologist and Esalen encounter group leader] had had to bring him out of it. So I decided I shouldn't try such a thing alone. But I would with Scott present soon. [Sept. 18, 1969]

I did not try going into trance even with Scott present. I never felt a Higher Self "green light" on that for me. And perhaps there was some Little Self fear, too, which was connected with past life experiences with the psychic dimension. In any case, I followed Higher Self directives in that realm, as I will share further.

In other experiences, usually following dreams, I felt Jim's presence physically—either in a warm tingling all through my body or in a vibrating kind of electrical energy that flowed through me and filled me. It was tremendously satisfying and comforting to have this physical sense of Jim totally present with me.

In still other dreams, I received information, or thought-messages. I was working during that time on the writing of *Search*. I had dictated the story onto tape, exactly as my mind had recorded it and with no interference from Little Self since she was still in shock. Then my brother Scott had transcribed the experience off the tapes so that I could bring the story into proper form for what turned out to be a book. One morning I awakened, having received an outline of information for a chapter to be included in the book, including its title, "Monotheistic Marriage." The information flowed onto the page in my dream log, and I felt I knew exactly what *Jim* wanted included over and above what I had already written in the book. On another morning a message received suggested a change in wording in a passage where I related a dream Jim had had about his mother. He indicated, "Change 'precognition' to 'premonition.'"

I had a sense of Jim's "approval" of *Search*. But more than that, I felt his participation in the writing of it. He had created opportunities during my dream states to add what he wanted to say, it seemed.

Shock as a Blessing

The time of shock was for me a time of blessing. In my Higher Self, I had an ongoing sense of communication and relationship with Jim which sustained Little Self on joy energy and a feeling that Jim was really O.K. and doing fine.

For my mind, shock was a time to record the memory of each detail of the Wilderness trek before Little Self's emotions were released to blur that memory. Those details were to become my book *Search*, finished only seven weeks after Jim's death.

For my body, there was an opportunity to work out much of its physical pains and to heal all its wounds (except for the tendons in my left ankle, which were two or three months in mending completely), in preparation for the new pain it would experience when the emotional suffering began.

For Little Self, shock was a period of giving energies over to tasks at hand: letters of condolence; Foundation business; estate matters; public appearances, including speaking engagements that Jim and I had made before his death and many of which I kept; a memorial issue of our little publication, *New Focus*; the writing of *Search*; and so on. In all of this I had much help and support, but had Little Self not been able to give her energies to the projects, I would not have accomplished all I did.

Shock lasted five and a half weeks for my Little Self. I am grateful that it did. Shock is a blessing bestowed on a Little Self not yet totally integrated with Higher Self, protecting her from feeling the full impact of her already suffered loss until certain physical and mental tasks of the Higher Self can be completed.

Shock must be difficult for family and friends to relate to in the bereaved person, for it delays the emotional responses people tend to expect. Yet if those who surround the one who grieves can also trust the process and affirm the person's needs, actions, and reactions during shock, then it will be easier for the one in grief to reach out to them again when the next phase begins.

I was very fortunate to be surrounded by family and friends who did not interfere with my processes during grief but rather affirmed me all the way along. While I was in shock, for example, no one mentioned to me that they were concerned about me, or felt I wasn't really facing the *fact* of Jim's death, or sensed that I was in shock. Instead, they simply affirmed me—my decisions, my lack of decisions, my actions, my reactions, my feelings—*receiving me as beautiful right where I was.* They stood beside me in love, confident that whatever was happening with me was right in that moment *for me.* I am very grateful for these affirmations, for they gave my Little Self the confidence she needed finally to face her pain and suffering.

We experience shock—sometimes called a delayed reaction—under many different circumstances and to greater or lesser degrees. If we welcome it as our total system's way of regulating the use of our Life Energies, then we can also welcome both the end of shock and the pain that follows.

4

SUFFERING

Little Self's Pain, Released

My journey through grief seemed timeless. I kept records of the dates of experiences and phases of experiences, but I was not oriented toward calendar and time-clock pinpointing. I felt as though I were walking through inner space in an encapsulated suit that functioned according to its own timing device. "Long" and "short" time periods did not have their former meanings. I was walking now in rhythm with my inner life pulse.

In comparison with other persons who have gone through grief, I spent a long time walking in shock. But there *is* no comparison, for each person has his own inner timing, and I was following mine.

One Friday evening, nearly five and a half weeks after Jim's death, I walked into our bedroom and experienced in my solar plexus a pain so severe that it felt as though someone or something had given me a hard blow to the middle. Simultaneously, the realization came in on my Little Self fully for the first time: "My God! Jim is *dead.*"

I was knocked off balance by the force of the realization and the accompanying pain. I stumbled in circles in the bedroom, holding my stomach and moaning, crying, sobbing, "Dead, dead, dead, dead."

The pain was excruciating. A metaphor emerged almost at once to describe what I was feeling. It was as though a huge tree had been growing in my viscera and someone had yanked it out by the roots, leaving a giant, gaping, bleeding hole in the "ground of my being." I later discovered that this same image has been used spontaneously by many others to describe the pain of losing a spouse or a child.

I clutched at my body in a futile attempt to ease the pain, as my Little Self—dazed by the awareness of the finality of the fact—kept saying over and over again, "Jim is *dead*. Dead, dead, dead."

There seemed nothing to do, nowhere to go. Not even the need to reach out. The energy transaction with myself was enough to absorb all my attention. That Little Self had not fully comprehended, or taken into herself, the *fact* of Jim's death, the utter finality of it, came into the light of consciousness. The intense pain that resulted was a shock that reverberated in my physical being with deep waves of pain.

Higher Self was lovingly observing and allowing Little Self to experience now what she had been protected from for five and a half weeks. Higher Self had lifted the insulation of shock. As the painful reality echoed through my being, my mind recalled an evening's session with Fritz Perls, father of Gestalt Therapy, at Esalen Institute in which Fritz had talked about the four explosions of life: anger, joy, orgasm, and grief. On that occasion I *thought* I had experienced the explosion of grief at the time of my grandfather's death when I was eight. But as a child, I had not known the depth of joy and sharing that were the opposite side of the grief coin, and thus could *not* have experienced the depth of pain and loss I was feeling now, though that had certainly been an explosion to the extent of my experience.

This realization opened the gates for Higher Self joy to

flood in alongside the intense pain in Little Self, for even Little Self could see that it was only because she had loved so deeply and completely that she was suffering so intensely what she viewed as the loss of that love. She saw that joy and pain were two sides of the same coin, and that both were evidence of fullness of life, of intensity of being, feeling, an interrelating.

As long as we continue to express ourselves through the physical body and the psychic nature, we will experience polarities of feelings, such as joy and pain, for the energy frequencies in the wave bands which correspond to this manifested plane are characterized by opposites. If we exchange energies with another through the generative center—by being sexually involved with, or giving birth to, someone, for instance— and the solar plexus—by having feelings for, about, or in relation to another—we leave ourselves vulnerable to the cessation of those energy flows.

When a person dies, he ceases to function in his physical body, thus cutting off the flow from the generative center, and generally he ceases to relate to persons still *in* the body on the feeling/thinking level (the psychic nature) as well. Some persons continue to relate "psychicly" (on the feeling/thinking level) after the death of their physical bodies, but unless the loved one left behind is able to register feelings and thoughts through extrasensory perception, such relating will not likely be consciously recognized and thus will be of little, if any, comfort.

What we call pain is actually a cleansing process. It is the clearing out of the remnants of the other's energy and the letting go (and perhaps this is the most difficult part) of the *patterns* of relating we had established with the loved one. We can no longer relate to the person physically at all, and if we want to have a relationship of a freeing nature, for both parties involved, we must find new ways to feel and think about them. Consequently, it is vitally important that we find new ways to channel our energy.* We will experience pain so long as there is any energy blockage in our being, or any "clinging" to the energy of the other. Grief is the process of releasing these energies.

This is where Higher Self can be of tremendous help. In the energy frequencies of Higher Self there is no discontinuity of relatedness, for at the Higher Self level we are one with the other, regardless of whether there is a physical body or a psychic nature involved. Therefore, resting in the steadiness of Higher Self, we are free to allow the cleansing to go on in the body, Little Self, and mind, and to guide the process of reintegration and the growth toward renewed wholeness.

One of my deepest learnings from the grief experience has been seeing the difference between *shock*, which insulates body, Little Self, and mind from almost all feelings and thoughts about the loved one, and *integration with Higher Self*, which enables body and Little Self to feel deeply and the mind to think its thoughts while staying in harmony with the way things are as Higher Self understands them in the big picture. In both cases pain is eased. In shock, it is because the pain is being delayed. In integration, it is because the feelings are in accordance with expanded consciousness of the nature of Life itself, and thus the feelings and thoughts are allowed to flow freely and be cleansed. They are *received as beautiful exactly as they are*.

Suffering Emotional Pain

I climbed into bed that Friday night and cried myself to sleep, going deeply into this new phase of grief. I was really *suffering* for the first time. There were no protections now. I was living with the whole of my being in the *full* awareness that Jim had died—that he was no longer on this plane of existence.

* For more information about the energy centers and channeling energies, see Diane K. Pike and Arleen Lorrance, *Channeling Love Energy*, San Diego: LP Publications, 1976.

When I awakened in the early morning, I was surprised to find the pain still intense and my legs aching unbearably. I had never experienced pain as severe as that which I entered as shock lifted. It was not physical pain. That is, the *cause* of the pain was not physiological. Yet I felt the emotional pain throughout my physical body with more intensity than any physiological ailment I had ever suffered.

Again I became aware of the integral nature of my being. What Little Self was feeling was totally reflected in my body. There was no separation in the manifestation, though the source or cause was different.

I lifted the telephone and called my friend Patricia Bradley in northern California. I woke her with the phone, and when she answered with a bleary "Hello?" all I could say was "Patricia? Help me!" I felt the phone to be a lifeline to Light. I burst into tears as I shared what had happened the evening before and my insight about the grief explosion. Patricia had been reading just the night before, in one of those noncoincidental examples of synchronicity, a book by Fritz Perls and had been struck by his observations on the four explosions. She shared with me out of that expanded understanding.

I told Patricia of my intense physical pain and of all my crying the night before. She suggested that perhaps the pain was my body's way of indicating that there was much more crying to do, and that perhaps I could give myself the gift of just being with myself and crying all I needed to. I now understand the deep wisdom of Patricia's words, for I am aware that pain and suffering are the result of blocked or unreleased energy, and I had obviously only just *begun* to release my emotional responses to Jim's death.

After we had talked nearly an hour, I thanked Patricia and hung up the phone. I felt she was right about the crying, so I completely let go and began to sob and moan and cry out loud in a torrent of pain.

My brother Scott had taken the fall quarter off from school—he was a junior that year at the University of California at Santa Cruz—in order to be with me in Santa Barbara. My family did not feel I should be alone either at home or while traveling. I kept many of the speaking engagements to which Jim and I had committed ourselves before his death, and these involved travel all over the United States. Scott lived in Santa Barbara and traveled with me all fall.

Scott was close to Jim and me before Jim's death and was working with us on our study of the historical Jesus. He lived with us for a quarter during his sophomore year, doing independent study in connection with our Christian Origins research. He traveled to Israel with us in May of 1968 and came to be with me, as the family's representative, during the search for Jim in the desert in Israel.

Thus Scott was close to me during some of my most joyous and some of my most painful life experiences. He became one of my closest friends, and the love we share goes far beyond affection between brother and sister. There is a deep soul bond as well.

Scott's room was downstairs, but he was awakened by my crying and came into my bedroom to see if he could be of help. Scott is a very gentle and tender being. He never intrudes by his presence but reaches out with the whole of himself, waiting to be invited into one's own life-space. "Diane," he said gently, "is there anything I can do?"

I motioned him over to my bed as I let his question run through my being. My legs were throbbing. "Perhaps you could massage my legs," I said. "They ache terribly." As Scott massaged, I went on crying. It was only much later that I learned about bioenergetics and Rolfing—techniques of therapy designed to release, through manipulation, massage, and physical exercise, emotional traumas stored in the muscles. Scott and I just went with the natural flow of what felt good, and what Scott did was to facilitate the release of pent-up emotional pain by massaging my legs.

And so began my suffering—a period of grieving that was to last ten and a half weeks for me but which felt like an enormous segment of the journey. There were many phases to the suffering, each of which seemed to last an eon and to consume huge quantities of energy. The journey through suffering offered me an opportunity to practice great patience with and love for myself. I learned to *receive myself as beautiful* no matter what state I was in—another of those principles for higher consciousness living.

Slipping into Depression

I had nearly completed the first draft of *Search* before I came out of shock, and I shall always be thankful for that. Once I began to suffer emotional pain, I had little leftover energy for anything creative. As a result, I almost did not finish the book.

Scott and I had gone north to Missoula, Montana, where I was to give a talk on the occasion of the first large nationwide Vietnam Moratorium Day march at the university there. I took the manuscript with me to begin revising the first draft while we traveled. As I read through the first chapter, I found it very boring and uninteresting. It consisted of all the details regarding how and why Jim and I went into the desert on that September day. The discouragement Little Self experienced at finding the first chapter so bad—not just in need of revision, but really uninteresting—immobilized her.

Because Little Self is the motivator, the dynamo that makes it possible for the whole of me to generate energy for action, when she shuts down her motors, there is little the rest of me can do about it. This is why depressions are so immobilizing. I depress my emotional energies, and there is no self-starter to get me moving. That's what happened that weekend.

I told Scott I was not going to do the book. It was no good. Scott, in his gentle, caring way, received me where I was. Gradually he got my Little Self to share what had happened. Then he asked, "How is the second chapter?" I hadn't read that far, so I had no answer.

Finally, on Sunday, I read the second chapter. It was fine.

It moved, it was interesting—even captivating. I shared that reaction with Scott.

"But I can't possibly revise the first chapter," I said. "I just don't have the energy."

"Then why not begin with the second chapter and throw the first one out?" Scott offered.

The suggestion came in so directly and with such clarity that it was as if a great cloud bank had lifted. "What a good idea!" I said. And how simple it was. By the next day I was able to begin work on the manuscript again, and within a week it was finished.

I share that slip into depression over the book as an example of a process I went through many times while grieving. As long as the days and nights went by relatively smoothly for me, I would get along all right, even if suffering. But when there was some kind of hitch, causing me to stop the flow of my emotional energy because there was a needed change of direction or a difficult decision to make, I would experience an intense drain of energy. It was as though by stopping the outpouring of energy, I prevented new input as well, and very shortly I would feel empty or exhausted. Such times of depression—when I was holding my energies down or in and did not see a way to get them flowing again—were very painful. Little Self felt she would never be able to move or act or accomplish again. And on most of those occasions she was not open to the suggestions of my own Higher Self either.

I found that usually it was the gentle, caring touch of a loved one's energies that revived Little Self and enabled her to get moving again. That's why it is so important to me in retrospect to realize that the gift my Higher Self *was* able to give Little Self during those times was that of reaching out again and again and again to family and friends for help when I needed it, *providing them with the opportunity to give to me.* They put me back in touch with my own Little Self energies.

Little Self felt the need to be physically held during that time. Higher Self kept telling her it was O.K. to ask. It was O.K. to receive. Many friends embraced me and held me close, and so did my parents and Scott and other family members. I found great comfort in physical contact, for it allowed my energies to flow again in the areas in which I was experiencing a cutoff because of Jim's death.

Reaching out for help and for touching had great meaning for me then as it does now. There was a time when I would not have asked for *or* received such gifts of love, because my mind would have told me that it was a sign of weakness to *need* to be held and that I had no right to draw on another's energies. *You should be strong,* was one of my mind's favorite messages.

But awareness of such self-denying attitudes came in on me during grief only as a distant memory of a life once lived in repression. These memories enhanced the life-affirmation, the self-affirmation, I was experiencing as I offered my needs and allowed them to be filled by loving persons who gave of themselves to me willingly, freely, even joyfully.

It was not until years later that I realized that just as I had intuitively shared my energies with Jim when his physical body was literally spent—dead—during the week of the search in Israel, so during grief I allowed friends and family to return that favor to me. The transferral of physical energies was truly lifesaving and healing to me during my grief.

The energy-drain experience continued long past the time of intense suffering, but it was then that I first became fully in touch with it, and it was then that I began to practice reaching out, asking and receiving.

Death Wishes

It was sometime soon after I came out of shock that my Little Self went through a time of fervent death-wishing. She wished she *had* died with Jim in the desert, and she wished she *would* die soon in the hope that she might still "catch up" with Jim and be with him once again.

Perhaps this was an inverse seeing by Little Self of the possibility of being with Jim and thus not suffering. Since she did not yet realize she could give herself lovingly and in total trust to Higher Self and thus *live* in that Oneness and unity, here and now, she imaged instead her own death as a necessary means to an end she felt to be possible—to be with Jim in spite of the death of his physical body.

Or perhaps it was my mind's limitations that did not permit Little Self's deep desire to go on feeling one with Jim to be translated into seeing that I still *was* united with him and that nothing had really been changed by the death of Jim's physical body. Certainly Higher Self knew that. But my mind still perceived a breach created by one physical body's being dead and the other's being alive. It still viewed Oneness as sameness of manifestation rather than as a state of consciousness.

My mind offered many fantasies of death during that time. Perhaps Little Self's favorite was that the long-predicted California earthquake would indeed come, and a giant tidal wave would sweep over Santa Barbara and wash me out to sea and to my death. Little Self lived many times in imagination the exhilarating feeling of taking a deep breath and riding that wave, in the undertow, to the other side of death, where she would be embraced by Jim and know the joy of his presence once more.

Another gift I, Higher Self, gave to my Little Self during this time was that of permission to talk about everything she was experiencing. I told her to hold nothing back. To share it all. She did. She used to share these death wishes and fantasies with Scott. He said many times that they worried him, frightened him. Higher Self would always reassure him: You needn't worry. That's how I *feel*, but I wouldn't do anything to bring my death about. It was important to keep the difference clear between my feelings (Little Self) and my intentions (Higher Self).

There was an important difference between these death wishes and the suicidal thoughts I had had in my adolescent years. The death wishes did not stem from self-destructive urges. They were Little Self's inverse expression of her joy in Jim and in the life we knew together. Because she so totally affirmed her life with Jim, she longed for it to go on in the magnificence she had known. She—because of her own emotional limitations and my limited mental concepts—did not see any alternatives to the death of her own physical body. It was not until nearly four years later that *she* moved from the inverse view of death to seeing it as it really is: a change in outer manifestation only, which in no way alters the *reality* of her Oneness with those she loves. Now she does not—and would not, during grief—need death wishes. She lives instead in the reality of joyful union, which is everyone's birthright.

Suicidal thoughts stemmed from quite another feeling. They were self-denying, self-hating, and escapist-oriented. They were my mind's suggestion on how Little Self could get *out* of the reality she knew rather than continue *in* that reality. The death wishes were life-affirmations viewed upside down. Suicidal thoughts were life-denials viewed from outside of self.

So it was easy for Higher Self to reassure Scott. Higher Self gave permission for Little Self to explore her feelings in their full intensity and to talk about them, but at no point did I allow Little Self to take over and run my life. Her feelings did not threaten to work against me/Life. Rather, they were an expression of my ongoing fullness-of-life experience.

Attempts at Communication with Jim

The pain was continuous, but sometimes it was more intense than at others. On the morning of November 2, the second-month anniversary of Jim's death, I awoke with such severe pain in my solar plexus region that I didn't know what to do with myself. My friend Rob Stuart was visiting that weekend, and he tried to comfort me, but his caring was not enough. I went down to Scott's room and awakened him. Then I just lay down beside Scott and moaned and cried for a long time while Scott quietly rested a steady hand on my back. I felt his being enfold me, and I was comforted, though the pain did not ease.

As the day wore on, I began to think that perhaps I should try to be in communication with Jim—that perhaps my severe pain was due to my failure to open myself to what he might want to say to me. This was perhaps my mind's attempt to rescue Little Self from her plight or at least to give her some relief, and my mind's "solutions" during grief were never very helpful. They intruded on the natural unfoldment of my inner processes.

I had had a few scattered experiences that felt as though they might be attempts by Jim to reach me since I had come out of shock—rappings on the wall in my bedroom, telephones or alarms ringing in my ear (but not in the "outer" reality) and awakening me, as examples—but in the main I had felt out of contact with Jim—a sign of my Little Self's loss of contact, temporarily, with Higher Self's ongoing relationship with him.

I had, from the time of Jim's death, received many, many letters from people across the country reporting that they had received messages from Jim. Most of the messages could not be verified or "identified" because of their general nature—e.g., "Tell Diane not to worry about me," or "Tell Diane I love her"—and I found no adequate way to feel about them.

My Higher Self affirmed that whatever the person had experienced was valid for that person. But my mind would frequently have a field day with unanswered questions that threw Little Self into turmoil: *Why do all these relative strangers get communications when I don't? Am I blocking*

Jim out? Am I closed? Am I too skeptical? Should I be doing something I'm not? Little Self felt insecure and sometimes anxious. She became defensive about "messages" relayed from others, feeling she had to fend them off in order to preserve her own sense of self-affirmation.

Higher Self managed to hold a fairly steady rudder during those stormy times when psychic waves were rushing in from across the country, but it was a time in which Little Self nearly fell into the waters of self-doubt and self-pity on many occasions. She had difficulty trusting that Higher Self knew how to navigate her life ship safely through the storm.

On this occasion I decided to invite close friends in for a time of prayer to see if we could reach Jim. That evening, Jim's mother, Pearl Chambers; and his aunt, Ethyl Larkey; John and Ellen Downing, Scott and I sat together in our living room and lifted our thoughts and prayers to Jim and for Jim. It was a meaningful experience for us all, and comforting to me, but none of us had any sense of direct communication.

I can see now that my cloud of emotional pain was so intense during those days that it would have been nearly impossible for me to receive anything directly, clearly, from Jim. What I was going through was a Little Self storm of emotion. It was a cathartic outburst that she needed to ride through, and until Higher Self had seen her through to clearer emotional weather, there was not much Little Self could receive by way of new information or input. Higher Self was being guided by radar (extrasensory perception and intuition), but Little Self was aware of almost nothing except what she felt. My mind's suggestion that she "should" communicate was of no help at all.

It was for that reason that I was grateful to be able to stand under the umbrella of family and friends who could shelter me from the storm without feeling the need to quiet it or pretend it wasn't there or give me advice about navigation through it. I was grateful for company and support, but

Higher Self knew that Little Self had to go through the darkness in order to find the Light in it. I did not want in any way to dissipate the energy or to suppress it. I wanted it to rage in all its intensity until it wore itself out.

Interaction with Dreams

There was only one occasion during those weeks of intense suffering when I felt that Jim was able to get something through to me. That came in a dream on October 31. My dream log reads:

Jim was writing a description of Esther in which he said he had gotten so he no longer even noticed what she looked like—not even what *he* looked like himself. He finished the description with "but Diane will be glad to know that I have forgiven Esther." I was glad because I knew it would be a relief to Jim. My immediate response was "Then I can forgive her, too."

That dream brought to me an inner healing of my vicarious feeling of Jim's inner wounds.

I had long been keeping a dream log and believed dreams to be gifts from my unconscious awareness to my consciousness. During grief I came to recognize fine differences in the primary energy-impulses or sources of the dramatized gifts given during sleep life.

Some dreams were occasioned by *physical states*—pain or sexual frustration or heat or cold. The images projected would be tumultuous, unordered, disorganized, and "gross" in quality—that is, unrefined and unclear. Upon awakening I would merely be in touch with the physical state reflected therein: I'm cold; I'm in pain; I'm sexually frustrated.

Other dreams were dramatizations of *emotions* seeking to make themselves known to my conscious awareness. During the weeks of suffering, my dreams were primarily of this nature. Always they were all-involving of me on the emotional level, leaving me with deep feelings on awakening. In the dreams, I felt that what was going on was *all mine*, and the other characters were there to meet a need of mine or to express a feeling of mine. These dreams were easy to gestalt, since I felt me in every part of the dream.

Still other dreams were somewhat like instant replays of events of the preceding day or days: video tapes, unedited and therefore jumbled together with no apparent cohesive feeling or unconscious intent. I always had a neutral feeling about such dreams on awakening, a feeling that they were not important but were just the mind entertaining itself with *memories*.

In some dreams I felt *Higher Self* to be revealing things to me, and I would awaken with a sense that something profoundly important had happened. Often such dreams end with a message that booms out in a loud, clear voice that awakens me; I still hear and feel the voice reverberating in my being on awakening. Other times I awaken with the thought, or message, summarized in one or two sentences for me, and I can then record it. I had no dreams of this kind until I was nearly out of the grieving altogether.

During grief I discovered a new kind of dream: that in which I was aware *in* the dream that I was dreaming and that the dream was being used as the context for *communication* with me by someone else. Not all my dreams of Jim were of this kind by any means, but on several occasions I knew *in the dream* that Jim was returning to be with me briefly, but that he would not stay long because he had died and this was a dream in which he had come to be with me. The quality of these dreams was entirely different from the kind sparked by unconscious feelings seeking to surface or to work themselves out in a dream state.

I received my dreams as gifts and interacted with them to learn what I could about myself. The result was growing understanding of the inner dynamics of self as well as an expanding perspective on the process of grief.

Finding a New Relationship to Jim

On November 6, while still in the midst of great suffering, I had the first dream indicating that, at some deep level, Little Self was moving into a new way of being with Jim—a new way of relating to him. This dream had elements of communication in it but dealt principally with feelings relating to him. My dream log reads:

This is the first night I have dreamt about Jim when he was back with me (*i.e.*, I knew he had come back after our thinking he was dead). There was no indication that he would leave again or that there was anything different [from before he died]. I simply cherished and treasured his being back, commenting on how hard it had been since he'd been gone. He was simply there—with nothing about death in the picture at all.

Otherwise in dreams I was put in rather frantic positions or situations and recognized them as such, but remained strong and calm and felt myself to be mature, even though I recognized the situation was frantic [because I was having to cope with Jim's death or impending death].

Again, on November 8, I dreamt:

A long dream in which Jim came back to stay. In the dream he appeared to have been gone about two weeks and it was as though the purpose of his going was to see what it was like and then to come back so he could tell everyone about it. I talked with him at length about the experience and he was able to tell me what it was like.

I asked if he was aware as he was passing over—if he could see what was happening. He said he was aware but he couldn't see very well and he was afraid he couldn't make it. So, he said, Jim, Jr., came and said he would help show him the way. He said he told Jim he didn't think he could make it and Jim said, "The hell you can't," and gave him a shove toward (I think) a car he was to drive. In the dream I was aware that that same image—driving a car—had been used in one of my earlier dreams to symbolize going on my own, and I thought *in the dream* that it was both a coincidence and a good symbol. I was impressed that his experience should have been like mine in that regard.

I asked if he was aware of us here when he was on the other side. He said he was. I was going to ask if he had been able to communicate with anyone but we got interrupted because (we were in my family's home in San Jose) we were all going to go somewhere and they were all waiting for Jim and me. First Mother said that my Aunt Helen was going to play the piano for us, so she sat down to play. It was as though she would play what she'd been practicing and then she could go on home and the rest of us would go where we were going. When she started to play, Jim went up behind her and started to place his hands over hers to play with her. I said, "Don't, sweetheart. She can't see when you do that. Play with Scott if you want." My eyes shifted to the left where Scott was playing a hymn. I had forgotten he played the piano and was surprised that he was playing so well, but I knew Scott would play with Jim and it would be O.K.

Before that Jim and I had been in the kitchen and the little bathroom. Jim was getting dressed to go. He went in to get a sweater and I was aware I had already given some of his clothes away. I remember thinking I could ask for them back—or maybe it was just as well I get him new clothes as he needed new clothes anyway.

I asked him if he had seen others he knew while over there. He said yes. I remember I had started asking questions because I knew as soon as we got with others they would start asking him things and I hated to learn the answers secondhand. Actually I would not have asked, myself, because it was enough for me to have Jim back. I was content and satisfied and filled with his presence and I knew with time he would share it all with me. But I started asking because we would soon start seeing others and they would ask. I just wanted to know first.

The import of his death seemed very clear in the dream. He had died in order to experience what it was like on the other side and to come back and tell about it. He was prepared to talk about it right away—like at the speech he was going to give on the night of his return—as though that's all he had gone for. And he was definitely taking me with him to tell about it. It's as though I could verify by giving testimony from my side that it was really true. I remember his saying, "So few are ever able to come back to tell about it." And I thought how few indeed there were who returned—and especially after so long a time when the vehicle of vitality had died and the soul and spirit bodies had actually departed from the physical body. I wanted to know all about that and to see if my experience [in the vision in Israel] had actually coincided with what had happened to him, but we didn't have time in the dream for me to ask him all of it.

I did have the definite feeling, though, that this is what we were to do together—we were to tell the story of what happened to Jim on the other side of death.

I had prayed intensely for understanding and guidance before going to sleep last night. Perhaps this is the beginning of it.

In this dream, there seem to be two levels of awareness operative at the same time: Little Self working toward a new way of being with Jim ("back to stay") and Higher Self awareness in the dream that it *was* a dream, noting especially the use of imagery (the car). It is possible that there are also elements of communication coming through here (what death was like for Jim, for example), but principally I see it as a Little Self dream in which I was finding my way to a new way to feel about Jim's death. The paragraph about playing the piano seems to indicate that though Jim was "back to stay" with us, what he did he would do with and *through* us rather than on his own and directly. Thus it was an entirely new relationship Little Self began to perceive: that Jim could be with us always—even though his body had died.

It is interesting to note that in this dream there seemed to be a clear indication that Jim would somehow tell of his experiences on the other side of death through me, or with my help as an interpreter. If that is a part of what he and I are to do together, it has still not unfolded—or at least not in the way implied in the dream.

What does seem clear at *this* distance (six years) is that there was a real sense in which Jim came back to me for good, or to stay. That is, I have felt him to be a real part of my ongoing life even though he is no longer with me in the flesh.

Responses Out of Phase

It was not until *eleven weeks* after Jim's death that I was able to completely relax my whole body. Perhaps I had released enough emotion by then that I was finally able just to let go.

This relaxation allowed me to experience, it would seem, the flood of painful emotion which hit me just two days later. It was November 21, and Thanksgiving was approaching, just five days away. I awoke with sharp pain in my viscera, and the pain increased all day. A deep fear began to come over Little Self that she would not be able to live through the holiday season—that is, that she would not be able to stand the pain.

The next day was a Sunday, and during Mass I asked out loud for prayers for Jim for the first time since his death. I had not been able before to gather courage to do that. I had been afraid I would break down in the middle of the request. After the service, as I was standing in the courtyard, a small boy—perhaps eight years of age—came up to me and asked, in the simplicity and unmasked clarity that only a child can manifest, "*Why* did you leave Jim alone in the desert?"

My Little Self screamed (inside) in pain, and it was all I could do to remain standing after the blow. It was as though with the precision of a surgeon's knife that child had cut through to the heart of my Little Self anguish. Higher Self rushed in with assurances that the child genuinely wanted an answer—information, that's all. Little Self has blocked my memory of what happened next—whether I gave an answer or not, and even who the boy was. All that Little Self permits to be released into consciousness is *that* the incident happened. So painful was it that she still has a "hold" on the full recall of the event.

The question that child asked is a clear example of a process of interaction I experienced quite often in grief. It has to do with being out of timing, or out of phase, with other persons.

I remember, for example, receiving a phone call from a mutual friend of Jim's and mine not long after I returned to Santa Barbara. I was still in shock and consequently not yet experiencing the disorientation of deep pain. Betsey began describing to me her own deep grief over Jim's death. My reaction on the feeling level was extraordinary: I felt *angry* at her for feeling the loss so deeply. After all, *I*, his wife, was not suffering deep pain; why should *she*, who was only a friend?

The fact was, of course, that Betsey was already deep into her suffering phase of grief, while I had not even come out of shock. But I had no way of knowing this.

On the other hand, there at the church was a little boy who had grasped an opportunity to ask me a simple question out of his own desire to know and understand. He was not in grief. He could have no idea that his question would cause me pain. He simply wanted information. But he just happened to put his question at a time when I was particularly vulnerable and raising a lot of questions for myself. Thus when I heard the question, I put it to myself on a much deeper level than the boy could have possibly intended, and I threw myself into deep pain with it.

Even though I often recognized in both my Higher Self and my mind that I was out of phase with people, still it was most difficult for me to handle such situations gracefully. Usually I just bungled through until I could get away by myself to deal with what was triggered in *me* by the interaction.

Perhaps it would be helpful if family and friends held in *their* awareness that often the grieving person is moving at a different pace and through different inner spaces than others are. Then they could be extra-understanding if the bereaved one has a "peculiar" response to a simple question or comment. This could be a special gift of gentleness to a loved one who is in pain.

Feelings of Rejection

I was in deep pain, and I was suffering the pain. On November 25, I awoke after the first of what I call my rejection dreams:

We were on a trip with a group of people. There seemed to be five of us. All of them had heard me tell what a great relationship Jim and I had, but Jim would pay no attention to me. When we stopped for the night, we got rooms and I just assumed that Jim and I would sleep together—naturally—in a double bed. I announced out loud that I was going to take a shower, thinking he would surely come and join me. He didn't. Finally I began to feel unwanted and unloved as I used to way back in high school and college sometimes. I started to go to bed by myself when one of the gals chidingly said something about our "loving" relationship. So I thought, *I mustn't let myself fall into this negative way of thinking—feeling sorry for myself and all.* Jim was lying in a double bed already. I went over and said cheerfully (as I have so many times), "Hi, darling," and started to climb in bed with him. He literally rolled out of the bed on the other side so I couldn't touch him. I crumpled down on the floor in a heap, crying out loud—sobbing. I really expected Jim would come to comfort me, but he didn't. Instead, a friend came and stood beside me, rather awkwardly, as though not knowing what to do or say. Jim stayed away.

When I awakened, I thought I could not stand the feeling of rejection, it was so intense. This was clearly my unconscious mind dramatizing for me my emotional response to being "left" by Jim. I had told all our friends about what a great and loving relationship we had, and then *he* refused to be with me by *dying* (which rolling off the bed on the other side seems to symbolize). He had literally left me alone in our marital bed, and others had had to come to comfort me.

I had accepted an invitation to have lunch with some

friends that day. I didn't feel like going, but my mind said I "should"—it would be "good" for me to be with people. I listened to my mind instead of following my inner feelings.

As I drove to my friends' house, Little Self was in a clear state of panic. She did not feel she could stand any more pain. She felt she would not make it through Thanksgiving. She dreaded going to my parents' home (where last year she and Jim had enjoyed a celebration with my family together), but she did not feel strong enough to stay in Santa Barbara and be alone either. She was in deep pain.

I sat down at the table while friends chatted, making small talk. Words bounced off my head. Little Self was so full of her own pain that she could absorb nothing. Finally lunch was served, and the hostess turned to me and said, "How are you feeling today, Diane?"

Little Self welcomed the chance to share her burden. With a rush of tears, she shared her fears about the holidays. Then she told of the rejection dream of that morning, with its deep impact. When she had finished, there was a moment of silence. Then my hostess said, "I'm sure Jim is up there somewhere saying, 'Why don't all those people stop feeling sorry for themselves!!' "

Remember that gaping, bleeding hole in the ground of my being? I had laid it open there, and her well-intentioned words were like heavy-cleated boots tromping through that hole, ripping, tearing, shredding, destroying.

My Higher Self fairly shouted at Little Self: *She didn't mean to hurt you!!* Here was another clear case of two persons out of phase with each other. But my Little Self had fallen bloodied into the gaping wound and was lying there sobbing, crushed and defeated. Higher Self nursed her through to the end of the lunch. Then I excused myself, nearly running out the door. As I drove home, Little Self tears kept blurring my vision, but Higher Self managed to stay in control—just. At long last, in the solitude of home, Little Self wept herself to exhaustion.

Scott had gone home for the holidays, taking a well-deserved breather from being with me. I was alone. I felt like going down to see Ellen Downing, but I knew she and John were planning to come up that evening, and my mind said I could wait. Little Self again listened to my mind.

That evening at about six o'clock an interview of Jim by Dr. Fred Mayer on educational TV was scheduled for re-broadcast. I planned to watch it. My Higher Self shouted again: *Don't watch that program alone!! Call someone to come to be with you.* Little Self was not listening. She was curled up at the bottom of her wound, hurting desperately, not willing to cry out for help. Momentarily she regressed to an old pattern of locking herself in her inner room, as though she could punish the friend whose words she had received as so hurtful by refusing to call on other friends to relieve her suffering.

The program came on. I watched it alone. An hour later, after being saturated with a false sense of Jim's presence, I snapped off the TV and my Little Self went into the hysteria of uncontrolled tears and screaming. She threw herself on her bed, pounding, screaming, tearing her hair.

Higher Self kept shouting, *Diane, call someone. Don't stay here alone! You are hysterical. Call someone. Do it now!!* But Little Self would not listen. She was drowning out her own Higher Self with screams and shouts.

Suddenly the phone rang. My Little Self had not heard, but other Higher Selves had. It was Jim's mother. She said, "Diane, are you alone?" Little Self could not answer through her tears. Pearl repeated, "You're alone, aren't you?"

"Yes!" I shrieked.

"Are you all right?"

"No."

"I'll be right there." She hung up.

Little Self collapsed on the bed again, screaming in her pain. *Call someone!* Higher Self commanded. Little Self heard. Jim's mother was in deep pain herself, and she was in her mid-eighties. The burden of a hysterical Little Self was more than even my Little Self wanted her to carry alone.

I crawled to the phone again and called the Downings. "John, it's Diane. Can you come, please?"

"We were planning to come anyway at eight."

"I need you now," I cried.

"We'll be right there," John replied.

I fell back on the bed in tears. The phone rang again. It was Gertrude Platt, my good friend and secretary. "Did you watch that show alone, Diane?"

"Yes," I answered weakly.

"I'll be right there."

The hysteria grew. Within a few minutes I was surrounded by loving, tender, caring persons. Mom Chambers, John, Gertrude, Ellen. They stayed with me, held me, put cold cloths on my head, talked to me.

My Little Self screamed and shouted—even angry at her little-girl God: *Why would God do this to us? Why did Jim have to die? Why, why, why?* (Questions fed her by my mind.) Some two hours later, my eyes swollen completely shut from crying, my friends put me to bed. Jim's mother crawled in bed beside me and stayed the night. The blackest hours of my grief had ended.

Diane K. and James A. Pike inside their Santa Barbara home, 1969.
Copyright © 1969, "Pictorial Living Magazine," San Francisco
Examiner

Diane K. Pike, R. Scott Kennedy, and James A. Pike, Santa Bar-
bara, 1968. Phil Oderberg

The canyon in which Diane Pike and James A. Pike were lost in the Judean desert. Arleen Lorrance

Diane Pike rests with searchers in a "cave" on the canyon slopes. David Rubinger from Black Star

Diane Pike breaks down during search for her husband in the wilderness of Judea. David Rubinger from Black Star

Diane Pike with James Pike's mother, Mrs. Pearl Chambers, at a press conference shortly after Mrs. Pike's return to the United States (San Jose, California, September 1969). Reprinted by permission of the San Francisco *Chronicle*

Requiem Mass for James A. Pike at Grace Cathedral in San Francisco, September 1969. Mrs. Pike reaches out to assure Bishop C. Kilmer Myers that it is "just right" that he officiate at the requiem. Left to right: John Charles (partially hidden) and Catherine (Pike) Patterson, Esther Pike (the bishop's former wife and mother of his children), Constance Pike, Bishop Richard Millard, Christopher Pike (partially hidden), Bishop C. Kilmer Myers, Diane K. Pike, and Mrs. Pearl Chambers (the bishop's mother). Reprinted by permission of the San Francisco *Chronicle*

Diane K. Pike, wearing both her own and her husband's wedding rings on her left hand, back at work in her Santa Barbara home, October 1969. Santa Barbara News Press

Memorial trip to Israel in January of 1970. From left: Pearl W. Chambers, Bishop Pike's mother; Diane K. Pike; and Ethyl Larkey, Bishop Pike's aunt, stand beside the gravesite at St. Peter's Protestant Cemetery in Jaffa. R. Scott Kennedy

Mayor Teddy Kollek of Jerusalem (on right) dedicates a playground park to Bishop Pike during memorial trip to Israel in 1970. Mrs. Pike is seated on the left. Y. Barzilay

Mrs. Pike unveils the dedicatory plaque as Mayor Kollek looks on, January 1970. Y. Barzilay

Diane Pike with her brother, R. Scott Kennedy, 1970. Hal Boucher
photo

*Diane Pike with Arleen Lorrance, with whom she is presently work-
ing in* The Love Project. Arleen Lorrance

James A. Pike and Diane Pike, 1969. Hal Boucher photo

5

SUFFERING
A Time to Love My Little Self

THE NEXT DAY I went to my parents' home in San Jose for Thanksgiving. My pain was still severe, but it was of some help to be able to share the fact of that pain with my parents, and to have them comfort me. All through my time of grieving I was continually aware of how fortunate I was to have my parents to give me the loving support I needed—and more important, to have parents who *gave* such support and comfort.

One morning while I was home for the holidays, I awakened after a painful rejection dream. I stumbled out to answer the door (I thought I had heard the bell ring). As I turned to go back to my bedroom, my mother met me. "What is it?" she asked. I told her about the door, and then suddenly the dream flooded into my consciousness and I broke into tears.

Mother took me into her arms and held me as I sobbed out the essence of the dream, telling her of my pain. Her only spoken words were, "I'm sorry you have to suffer so much." Her warm embrace said everything else that was important.

I have often thought how wise my parents were during that time and how fortunate I was to be the recipient of their loving wisdom. Mother could have told me on that occasion all the reasons why I shouldn't feel the way I did. Instead she gave me the free gift of her love, and that was what—that was all—I needed.

Thanksgiving day was difficult, but my family understood. Late in the afternoon when the pain was severe and I felt I had to get out of the house, I put on a coat and said I was going for a walk. My sister Jean unobtrusively said, "May I walk with you?" She did just that. I don't remember if we even spoke as we walked. It was that kind of being beside me that gave me such strength through those difficult days.

Before I entered the painful rejection period, I had set up a series of meetings in the San Francisco Bay area for the week after Thanksgiving. I wanted an opportunity to tell Jim's closest friends the story of what had happened to us and to provide them with the opportunity to ask whatever questions they wished. The newspaper accounts of the search for Jim, and of our trek into the Wilderness, had been confusing, incomplete, and often contradictory, and almost everyone who felt a deep involvement with Jim and his life was left feeling unsatisfied.

As the time for these meetings approached, my Little Self was in such deep pain that she did not want to be with people. Her feelings of being rejected by Jim grew, and she began to feel unlovable in general because of being unloved by Jim. My dream log entry of December 2 expresses very well what my Little Self was going through:

We were at a big conference of some kind. . . . We went into a room with a fireplace—a lounge type room—and Jim was there. A woman was also there with whom I knew Jim had been intimate. I first turned to her to invite her to sleep with us. Then, as if remembering that Jim hadn't slept with me for a long time, I turned instead to him and said, putting my arms up to his shoulders, "Sweetheart, won't you please sleep with me?" He shook his head "no." I turned to the other woman as though feeling she might somehow be the solution and said, "You could sleep with

116

us," but it was apparent that Jim wasn't going to sleep with me. Then Scott walked up and said, "Mother said she's going to go with us for the weekend," as if that would reinforce what Jim was saying—that he wouldn't sleep with me. I turned to Scott and shouted, "I don't care if she is. Jim is my husband and I guess I have a right to sleep in the same bed with my husband if I want to." I started crying, but Jim did nothing, so I turned toward the fireplace and, sobbing, started to take off both my wedding rings [I was wearing Jim's ring with mine after his death] to throw them in the fireplace. But after I got them all the way off, I thought, *No, I don't want to do that,* so I put them back on. Then I woke up.

I want Jim back so much—not for Jim's sake at all but just very selfishly for myself. I loved him more than I thought it was possible to love anyone. It's so hard to let him go. I know he's dead, but I don't *want* him to be dead. I want him back here with me. I don't see how it will ever be possible to learn to live without him again. In spite of how illogical it is and how uncharacteristic of Jim, I feel rejected by him. I feel less lovable in general, less attractive. It's as though no one could ever love me again now. If Jim doesn't love me, who could?

Higher Self watched all of this and monitored my mind's interplay with Little Self. The mind kept waiting to marshal all kinds of logic and evidence to prove to Little Self she had no right or reason to feel as she did. Higher Self would not allow such passing of judgment. Whether it was logical or not, whether she had any "right" to or not, Little Self was feeling Jim had died to get away from her. Higher Self knew that however illogical the feelings, if Little Self didn't stay with and in her feelings till she no longer felt them, the unspent, unreleased energies caught up in those emotions would eventually cause her trouble. Higher Self preferred to stay with the pain now in order to have no residuals later.

Little Self began to say that Jim's friends did not really want to come to the meetings that had been set up and were coming only out of a feeling of obligation and that none of them really wanted to hear what she had to say. Higher Self was able to hold her gently and lovingly and to say, *I can understand the pain you are feeling and I know you are feeling unloved and unlovable, but you are not the one who will be talking to Jim's friends. You have no evidence that they do not wish to come, and just because you are feeling rejection does not mean you can lay the rejecting on them. These are not your meetings. You will just have to bear with me while I tell the story again, and then I will be back with you. But you may not interfere with these gatherings, and you may not take control of my life.*

Being a loving parent to my Little Self was easy, as Higher Self had a broad perspective on what was going on. Not only could I give Little Self the support she needed and help her to find comfort, but I could also set limits on her so that her pain and grief did not rule my life. Higher Self kept a balance in my experience during those days and weeks and months so that I did not lose touch with reality.

Being with Myself in Sexual Frustration

It was during the period of rejection feelings that I also experienced the height of my sexual frustration following Jim's death. I had been a virgin when I met Jim, and in the course of three short years had come to know total fulfillment of my being, including a rich and very active sexual life. Then suddenly Jim was gone, and I went from plenteous sexual activity to a sexual frustration that felt like starvation.

Part of what made my life with Jim so rich and satisfying was that we met each other and gave ourselves to each other on every level of our beings. Sexual intercourse was just one expression of the totality of our union, and the climax of orgasm was just one outlet for the ever-surging energy we shared with each other—the explosions of fulfillment we felt over and over again in the course of our days together.

When Jim's body died, our union on the physical plane

was cut off, and there is no question that my physical body registered the impact of that separation. I could feel—literally—the reality of the Biblical adage that two become one. Someday scientists will be able to explain that phenomenon, but as I sense it, it is that there is a commingling of the atoms of our beings in every dimension: physical, emotional, mental, and spiritual (to use four possible descriptive labels).*

When Jim's vital energy was withdrawn from the physical and emotional levels, as I experienced it I suffered withdrawal pains. I am sure this is what the image of the uprooted tree symbolizes. We had rooted our lives in each other, both physically and emotionally. To *uproot* that union on those levels caused me great pain. I have come to see in the last year or so that it is because of that physical and emotional rooting process that the universal love of Jesus—and of others like him, such as Gandhi and Schweitzer—was not expressed sexually or emotionally.

I also felt the lack of energy replenishment, which had been so much a part of our relationship. We felt it twenty-four hours a day. We were totally open to each other, and the energy that was flowing into each of us from the cosmos flowed constantly *between* us as well. We were getting, in effect, a charge and recharge at the same time.

This was why we not only *could* be together all the time but *preferred* it. Not only was there no *drain* in that twenty-four-hour association, but the replenishment was inherent in it. Jim and I often commented on how unusual it was for two people to prefer "togetherness" as a steady diet. Our previous

---

* Surely a comparable experience is that of a mother who loses a child by death. The atoms and molecules of the mother's being have literally been given to the child as a gift of life. The child's body and being have lived *in* the mother's body for nine intense months and then have taken of her very essence—a portion of her physical and emotional body—in order to be born into this life. It is no wonder, then, that when a child dies, a mother feels that something of her own self has died with it. In the most basic sense, this is true. The resultant physical and emotional pain is excruciating.

patterns (this is typical of most Aquarians, and we were both born under that sign) had been to seek, want, and *need* time alone, time apart, even from those whom we loved the most.

After Jim died I was able to meet my emotional needs fairly well by reaching out to and receiving from loving family members and friends. My sexual needs were another story, however. My appetite was large in those early months, as I was used to a regular and abundant diet. Sources of fulfillment were few and scattered.

I no longer held mental convictions that it would be "wrong" to fill my sexual needs. Rather, I felt physical needs to be as natural and healthy and normal as any other needs I had. The question was not *whether* to fulfill them but how and with whom.

I gave myself the gift of experimentation—a gift I had not given myself during my dating years—so that Little Self could learn consciously and directly how she felt about sex now, in the aftermath of such a fulfilling union. Over the course of a seven-month period of time, from November to May, there were several occasions on which I chose to be intimate with someone. The most meaningful of those sharings were with a man who was a close friend of both Jim's and mine and who gave me more than sex in his warmth and love and understanding; and with another man whom I found very attractive and exciting in every way, and thus shared fully with in ways other than, or in addition to, the sexual.

Other encounters ranged from sexually exciting, to sexually exhausting, to pleasant but not very exciting, to more frustrating and unfulfilling than not having had sex at all. Perhaps a better way to express it would be to say that the other encounters *were* "having sex," not making love, and thus were fulfilling, if at all, only in that one dimension of my being and thus only briefly.

By May of 1970, I was back to the feeling I had had before I met Jim—that to be sexually involved just for the meeting of physical needs was not fulfilling enough for me to warrant the accompanying emotional and relational entanglements, and thus was not something I would choose in and of itself. I came to that decision from experience this time, not from the lack of it. I knew more fully than ever that the physical is an expression of my whole being; therefore its fulfillment, or need of gratification, could not be separated from the whole of me. My body does not govern me by its needs; rather, it serves as an expression of me and I determine how its needs will be met. I knew there were avenues open to me *other than* sexual activity for the fulfillment of my physical needs, and once again I opened myself to the discovery of those other channels of creativity and expression.

The healing of that gaping wound caused by the wrenching of the atoms of Jim's physical and emotional being out of my energy field came, then, not by my *replacing* Jim with another man, sexually or emotionally. It came instead through my discovery of a new kind of wholeness within myself. I grew to discover within my own nature those qualities that Jim had represented for me in my life. I grew to be consciously aware of my masculine, as well as my feminine, nature, and began to experience an inner marriage equal in depth and profundity to the outer union I had shared with Jim. Thus, in my sexual "frustration" lay one of the greatest opportunities offered me by grief. By engaging with that frustration, I came to some of my most profound learnings.

From Rejection to Guilt

On December 6 the pain began to ease some. Two days later I had another of those rejection dreams in which Jim spent the whole dream avoiding me and trying to get away from me. As the dream approached the end, I realized Jim was going to die as his final resort—just so he wouldn't have to be with me and sleep with me. Little Self must have allowed Higher Self insight into the dream, for some part of me saw what was coming and asserted, in the dream, No. *I will not finish this.*

That had to be Little Self. I woke up. I knew then that the rejection syndrome was ended.

This was the first example I had of the working-through of feelings in a dream state. It was for Little Self a confirmation that Higher Self was right: if she went *through* all the feelings instead of avoiding them because of the pain, eventually the energies would neutralize themselves, or burn themselves out, and Little Self would not need or want to go on feeling them at all. The whole self—the human system—has its own internal processes of communication and self-regulation, and if allowed to go through its own processes without interference, it will find its own balance of energies again and carry out its own healing. If the mind interferes by being judgmental and repressing feelings, then blockages and short circuits can occur, causing complications that could take years to repair. Little Self was grateful for the wisdom of my Higher Self in letting her go through it all just as the feelings emerged.

Only shortly thereafter, Little Self feelings of rejection became transmuted into feelings of guilt. A series of dreams began in which I was searching for Jim in the desert and was unable to find him. Someone in the dream (my mind's spokeswoman) would begin moralizing, telling me I *should* have done more and it was my fault he had died. The dreams were so painful that, upon awakening, my Little Self would feel desperate, not knowing how to cope.

Higher Self continued to watch Little Self in her handling of Little Self's grief work. In *Up from Grief** the authors report that nearly everyone who has lost a mate or a child goes through a period of guilt, feeling responsible for the death either by fault or default. Higher Self knew there were no data to justify my Little Self's feelings, but that didn't alter her sense of guilt.

* *Up From Grief: Patterns of Recovery,* by Bernadine Kreis and Alice Pattie, New York: The Seabury Press, 1969.

Finally the pain began to ease some. One morning, in mid-January, I awoke, having had one of the most fascinating dream experiences in my memory.

I was in the desert helping in the search for Jim. A woman [my mind] followed me and engaged in an ongoing, highly judgmental commentary all the while. She kept telling me I wasn't doing enough or trying hard enough. Finally I came to the place in the canyon where Jim's body was actually found. I looked across and saw him lying there in the burning sun, suffering terribly. The searchers who were with me could not get to him, so I began to call to Jim from across the canyon. I explained that we were there and were doing all we could; that he was in a very difficult place and the searchers could not get to him but that they would keep trying; that the reason he was suffering so much was that the heat was about 140 degrees; that dying of the heat is very painful because of the effects of dehydration on the body and that perhaps he could draw on my strength and love, knowing I was there with him.* I was weeping in agony as I called to Jim, my heart aching beyond conception. Then the judgmental woman spoke from behind me, saying, "You *should* have been able to save him." I took hold of her by the hair, lifted her up and shook her mercilessly, shouting, "Judge not that you be not judged! Until you have the facts—until you know what really happened— you should not judge." Then I threw her down on the ground and woke up.

At first I was astonished at the vehemence with which I had lifted that woman up, shouted at her, and thrown her down. Then the awareness dawned that this was my Little Self's way of refusing to go on with the guilt feelings, of throwing them off. I was proud of her and delighted for her. Another phase of grief had ended, I knew, and Little Self had

* For a description of what actually happened when the searchers found Jim's body, see Diane K. Pike, *Search*, New York: Pocket Books, Inc., pp. 133–42. It was not unlike what I describe here except that Jim had already died and it was Scott, not I, who was with the searchers in the canyon.

moved to a new level of self-affirmation, though not yet without pain.

Loneliness and Isolation

Somewhere in the midst of the guilt feelings, Little Self went through a period of feeling completely cut off, isolated, and without moorings—adrift in a large, dark sea. This was a time of darkness, of depression, and of a heavy, pressing kind of pain that was interspersed with the more clear-cut feelings of guilt.

Higher Self gave Little Self the gift of taking her home to her parents during that time of feeling cut off, for surely there, if anywhere, she could rediscover her lifeline, the secure ground in which she stood firmly rooted and from which she drew unending nourishment.

I described the awful dreams I had been having, the guilt, the flashes of Jim on that cliffside that came to me often even during the day, and my sense of isolation. Mother and Dad listened compassionately, saying little. Then Dad invited me into the den to sit with him for a while. He put his arm around his little girl as we sat on the couch, and he talked to me quietly for a time. Then he said, "Just a moment," and left the room.

Another of Dad's sure-cure remedies for pain when we were growing up—if it wasn't crackers and milk—was finding something to distract our attention from what hurt. He did it by a magnificent undersell technique he had developed. Soon Dad reappeared carrying a basket of Christmas cards. He sat down beside me and took out a card. "Here are some Christmas cards we've received," he began. "I don't suppose you remember the Watkinses."

My Little Self recognized at once that we were playing the distraction game, and she settled into it as one slips into an old slipper for comfort. If Higher Self can smile, she did so then, for I saw a loving father rescuing his little girl again.

Each card he picked up, he said, "I don't suppose you will be interested in this," or "You probably don't know these people." Each time Little Self protested that she was interested, she did know. Finally, Dad put the basket on my lap and left. Like an obedient child, I sat, looking at and reading each card in the basket. I was finishing the lot when Dad reappeared at the door.

"I just went into the dining room, and your mother asked me where you were. I told her you were in the den reading Christmas cards. She said maybe you didn't feel like reading Christmas cards." He paused. Then he went on, the fully conscious adult speaking: "I never thought to ask you."

Of course not, my Higher Self said, *because you were intuitively being the good father to your little girl. You did just what she needed. You helped her tap into her roots again.*

Just before Christmas, the worst of the pain of suffering began to lift. On the twenty-third I was due in Los Angeles to do a television show. As I drove down the freeway, there surged within me a sense of future for the first time. I caught a glimpse of a me without Jim. I had a sense that I could make it on my own, that there was something important for me to do. With that first glimpse of the future came the end of "pure" suffering and the beginning of recovery, as I experienced it.

I had spent five and a half weeks in shock; the time of deep suffering had lasted ten and a half weeks. Just four months after Jim's death, then, I had already begun my recovery. It had been "only" four months, but it felt as if a major portion of my life had passed.

6

RECOVERY
The Balance of Energy Shifts

THE LENGTH of the various segments of my journey through grief are measured in my memory not by their duration but by their intensity. With the beginning of 1970, I experienced a shift of energy. No longer was the intensity weighted almost entirely on the pain side, but a new balance began to emerge. I shifted back and forth between pain and hope, weakness and strength, past and future, almost as though I were walking from one end to the other of a teeter-totter within. Occasionally I would stand at the midpoint and know the balanced energy of integration. Then I would walk out onto the energy seesaw again and experience the pulsation and fluctuation. I was discovering that my perfection lies both in the balance and in the end points of experience.

That portion of the grief experience which I call recovery passed more quickly for me than the suffering, even though it was much longer when measured by days and weeks. A growing inner strength no doubt accounted for my sensation of more-rapid progress.

The Return Trip to Israel

Before Jim's death, he and I had planned to lead a study tour to Israel in January of 1970. My brother Scott and I decided to go ahead with those tour plans, making it a memorial journey for friends and family. On January 17, 1970, Scott and I set out with a group of thirty-two persons on a Bishop Pike Foundation Memorial Tour of Israel. Among the group were Jim's mother and aunt, Scott's and my parents, one of Jim's biographers, several other close friends of Jim's, Scott's, and mine, and a group of persons who had known and admired Jim in a variety of contexts.

That tour was my first return to Israel after Jim's death. Strong anxiety set in before we left. I had fantasies of plane crashes, of my parents or Scott dying in Israel, and of our tour group getting lost.

I felt it was important to go back. I kept thinking of the years when I was a swimming instructor. I had found that if someone did a belly flop while learning to dive, or had difficulty in the water while swimming, it was important for them to go back at once and try again. If they waited even a day, the fear induced by the experience could crystalize to such a degree that it was often difficult ever to get them into the water, or onto the diving board, again.

I knew that something like that could happen to me. If I did not return to Israel, where I had had such a traumatic experience, I might always fear going back, or *any* foreign travel, for that matter. It was with a determination to be free of all fear that I was returning.

A few days before we left on the tour, Scott and I were invited to dinner at our friends the Meynets. Maryanne and Alain Meynet had been especially helpful to me after Jim's death, because they made clear that they would gladly do anything they could to be of help and then simply went on relating with the natural ease of friends who loved and cared for me. They extended invitations to me the same as they would have extended them if Jim had still been alive.

On this occasion, they wanted to be with Scott and me before we went on our tour. Over dinner, Maryanne asked how I was feeling about the prospect of returning to Israel. Tentatively, I began to explore the fears I had been having. Then Scott shared his—which were not unlike my own—and the two of us finally brought into the light of consciousness, in the warm presence of loving friends, dreams and fantasies we had had but had not talked about before for fear they would become realities.

Instead, the reverse was true. By expressing the energies in words, we gained control over them and were able to release them as what they were: fears and fantasies. In this way we were able to move on from them, having freed ourselves from them. To release fears by verbalizing the energy—thus bringing it into consciousness, where it can be rechanneled—is to make room for other energies to begin to flow again.

The night before we were to leave, my suitcases were all packed and my room clean and tidy before I went to bed. When I awakened in the morning, my slippers were strategically placed in the passageway to the bathroom so that there was no possible way I could miss seeing them.

I was startled at first, because I knew they had not been there when I went to sleep. Then there swept over me a feeling that this was a sign from Jim that he would be with us on the tour—that he was near.

I called Scott to come and see the slippers, and we both made notes of the manifestation. We felt warmed by what appeared to be a "sign" from Jim.

The very first event of our trip was a visit to St. Peter's Protestant Cemetery in Jaffa, where Jim's body is buried. This seemed an appropriate pilgrimage for a memorial tour to make, and all the more moving because of the persons who were present. For Jim's mother, now eighty-five years old, it was a moment of truth not easy for her to bear. As she viewed it, her son was buried "alone" in a foreign land. She wept for her own sense of loss as her sister Ethyl and I stood beside her, our arms linked around her.

For my parents, it was an opportunity to be present, even though months after the fact, with Scott and me in what had been a time of deep pain for all of us. And for Scott and myself it was an opportunity to share with family and friends a visible reminder of those events that had so altered our lives just four months before.

On the grave stood a white wooden cross, placed there by the caretaker, who said it had not seemed right to have no marker at all on the grave of such a famous man. (The gravestone could not be laid until a year had passed and the ground was firmly settled.) We placed our roses before the cross and said silent prayers for Jim's peace and our own healing.

One of the joyful aspects of our memorial trip was that we were privileged to be present for two special ceremonies in tribute to Jim. The first was the dedication by the city of Jerusalem of a playground park in Jim's name. Called The Bishop Pike Garden, it is located in an immigrant development in the northern sector of East Jerusalem. Mayor Teddy Kollek presided over the dedication. And the other ceremony was planned by the Jewish National Fund, which had dedicated an entire forest of 10,000 trees in Jim's memory. Many of us had made contributions to a memorial fund that had purchased trees for the forest, and it was a special joy to be there for the unveiling of the marker for The Bishop Pike Forest.

There were difficult moments on the tour—times when I had a great deal of pain—but on the whole the trip had a healing effect. By the time I returned to the United States again, in February of 1970, I had a new sense of strength and integration.

It was while I was in Israel that my first strong sense of

direction emerged. While we were staying in Tiberias on the Sea of Galilee, a clear directive came in on me one morning: *Return to Israel to spend six months.* I shared that thought-message with Patricia Bradley, with whom I was rooming, and then with Scott. And I sent back the thought many times that I would gladly come, and would know if it was right for me to do so, if plans worked out easily so that I could. It has been my experience that Higher Self directives come into manifestation effortlessly, because they contribute to and are part of a larger harmony of which my life is a part. One way of knowing whether guidance is from Higher Self is to see if doors open or close along the indicated way. In this case they opened.

Communicating with Jim

On our way home from Israel, Scott and I stopped in London with the intent of seeing Mrs. Twigg, the medium who had contacted Jim during the week of the search (on the Thursday night when Jim had not yet left his rapidly decaying body), and who had, on several occasions from 1966 to 1968, been able to bring Jim, Jr., through to his father. We also wanted to see several scholars we hoped we could consult with in our undertaking to complete the book on the historical Jesus.

We had two sittings with Mrs. Twigg during our stay in London. On neither occasion did we feel the communication to have been directly from Jim. In fact, at the second of those two sittings, I had such a strong sense of Jim's presence in the room that I kept feeling he might get through to us if Mrs. Twigg would just stop talking! We also sat with another medium while we were in England, and that experience was even further from satisfactory.

Those occasions were the only ones after Jim's death on which I sought communication with him by sitting with a medium. I did not really feel the need for such assistance, for

I had my own ongoing sense of union with Jim through my Higher Self, and I also had dreams and other experiences of communication.

Emotional and Mental "Static"

I also felt that there was much "interference" in the air because of all the interest and curiosity that Jim's own reported experiences with psychic phenomena had stirred up. I received many inquiries from the interested and the curious, not the least of whom were members of the press, about whether I had been able to communicate with Jim. Many, many sensitives and mediums—professional and lay—were eager to prove they had been contacted by Jim or had been chosen by him as "the" vehicle through which he would communicate. Many of the latter had contacted me by mail or phone. It was my feeling that the emotional investments that people had in being able to *prove* that Jim could communicate were so intense as to cloud the channels of clear vision or hearing through which Jim might have sent messages.

Certainly *my* channels were clouded most of the time. The grief I was experiencing was entirely my own process and not one with which Jim could be of any more help than people who were here beside me. I *knew* (Higher Self certainty) that Jim lived on and was still in union with me on some level. Thus I felt communication continued between us. But I also knew that my grief had to do with adjusting to life *without* him on this physical plane and that constant "contact" with him might not only not help in this adjustment but might even delay it in the long run.

Moreover, I was sure Jim had many adjustments of his own to make. Before his death, people often asked Jim if he believed in reincarnation. He would answer that he was a one-world-at-a-time kind of guy. That he was coping now as best he could. He figured that, whatever there was, he would cope with that, then. I did not want to distract him from his coping. I wanted him to be able to give himself fully to *his* present moment, while I coped with mine.

One other important factor was that I did not feel we had any unfinished business between us. We had made a practice of sharing everything we were thinking and feeling in the moment, so we were always up to date with ourselves. I could not think of one more thing I would have asked him or said to him if I had had an opportunity before his death. Therefore, I did not feel a need to get in touch with him in order to clear up any misunderstanding or resolve any leftover feelings.

This contrasts with Jim's own experience, for example, in which he had had many unresolved feelings and many questions following his son's death by suicide and thus found communicating through a medium—one who was experienced in such contact—very helpful. In many reported instances of communication, unfinished business is said to be the motivation or impetus for the contact, as it was between Jim and his son. That factor was missing between Jim and me.

The Process of Communication

Often persons in grief have asked me to whom they might go to communicate with their loved one. There are, of course, hundreds of psychics who might be able to make such a contact. There is no way I could possibly know of all of them, nor do I feel I can recommend persons with whom I have not personally sat.

What I do like to stress is that communicating with persons no longer in their physical bodies is very much like communicating on this plane. That is, when you express a thought—verbally or nonverbally—there is never a guarantee that the one who receives that thought will understand what you meant to communicate. Even if a person *hears* your words, he interprets them according to his own understanding and frame of reference.

If, then, there is a third person involved—a mediator

(medium) through whom you are seeking to communicate—the process is made doubly complex. The medium registers a thought, understands it according to his own frame of reference, and puts it into words for you. You then interpret the words according to your understanding. Under these circumstances, communication is often spotty and sometimes frustrating and disappointing. Sometimes, also, it is fluent and clear.

If you go to a sitting with *no expectations,* you will not be too disappointed if the mediumship of a given individual does not provide you with the contact you longed for. Moreover, if you do not limit your sense of *expectancy* about the channels through which such ongoing relating might be carried on, then you may be rewarded time and again with the sense that you have been and are still linked in consciousness with the one you love. In other words, communication through a medium is *only one way* in which you might experience your ongoing relationship with a loved one.

Under all circumstances, it feels important to me to realize that *you* are the only one who can judge what is a true and valid experience *for you.* Its meaning lies in the significance you give it. Whether others agree or disagree is of no relevance to your ongoing pattern of growth.

Seeking Advice

Often people have asked if I have sought Jim's guidance or advice, or if he has been helping me in my endeavors. Again, the one-world-at-a-time philosophy is relevant, for I feel I have my work to do and Jim has his. Mixing the two "worlds" might prove to be a deterrent to the progress of both of us. Though there have been ways in which I have felt Jim's involvement in my ongoing life and work, I have never actively *sought* such guidance.

I have never been one to seek advice. I have a deep knowing that when I make decisions, I am responsible for them and no one else is, even if I am following someone else's advice. I often talk things over with others, but when I make up my mind, I do what feels right to me. I did not ask Jim for guidance *before* his death, nor was I prone to afterward.

Because this is my way of proceeding in life, I have been surprised—even shocked—as I have become somewhat acquainted in psychic circles, to find that there are many people who take the advice that comes to them through mediums as though that advice were law—or straight from "God Himself."

One evening I was invited to the home of a woman interested in parapsychology to meet some of her friends. One of the persons present was a medium, and at the hostess's request he agreed to demonstrate his gift. While this gentleman from Scotland was purportedly in trance, his guide spoke through him from the other side of the veil we call death. He gave messages to many in the room, but since I did not know anyone there, I had no way of knowing how valid the messages were. I do know that each time he spoke to me, he said nothing that meant anything at all to me, and what he said about Jim was either irrelevant or false. I was very unimpressed with his abilities as a psychic and certainly unconvinced that his messages were in any way from "the other side."

One of the women present asked him, while he was "in trance," "Can I trust my business partner?" The answer she got was "No. He is untrustworthy. You should by all means let him go. The sooner the better."

"But," she said, "I am about to leave on a trip to Europe, and I am leaving him in charge of everything."

"If you want to have anything at all upon your return, you should surely let him go now" was the medium's reply.

The woman was greatly distressed, and at the end of the sitting she went on at great length about how she would obviously *have* to let her partner go, but she didn't see how she would manage.

I was amazed that she would have taken the word of the medium or an unknown entity—if indeed he was that—as authoritative for her. If she had doubts about her partner serious enough to warrant his dismissal, then the advice that came through the medium might have served as a confirmation for her. If she didn't, then that she would act on that advice was inconceivable to me. When advice is a confirmation of what I already know, that's one thing. When it comes in as an incongruous or disturbing thought, to follow it would be to go against my own center of knowing.

There have been ways in which I have felt Jim's participation in my newly chosen work. However, most of this did not begin until grief was long over and I had begun to follow my own path in accordance with my inner promptings. It seems significant to me that our sharing together as partners in a *new* way, in the new dimension of relationship we have now, did not begin to emerge until I had finished grieving for the loss of the *old* relationship. Grief work was my Little Self's task, principally; the work Jim and I were and are engaged in is Higher Self oriented and directed. The latter had to wait until the former was cleared away.

Direct Messages from Jim

On occasion I have had reason to want to communicate directly with Jim. In each case, I have done so knowing that I have an open line of communication whenever I want to use it. One such occasion arose in February of 1970. The twenty-one-year-old son of our good friends Peggy and Keith Kerr died of cancer. Not being sure whether or not Jim would be aware of Russ's passing over to the other side, I sat down in meditation as soon as I learned about Russ, and concentrated on what I wanted to tell Jim: "Russ has died. Please be there to meet him and help him make the adjustment."

I held that single thought for a long time—perhaps half an hour, or an hour. Then came a clear response in the form of a thought that dropped into my consciousness: "I know

Russ has died. It is not my role (function, place) to meet him and welcome him, but once he has made the adjustment I will be able to talk with him."

The answer was as clear as if I had been talking with Jim on the telephone. So clear was it that I immediately phoned Peggy and Keith to tell them what Jim had "said." Since they had been with Russ as he made his transition, aiding and encouraging him to leave his decayed body and move out and into the Light, they received the message in the same simplicity with which I offered it, sharing my certainty that communication is not only a possibility but a reality.

There was another occasion, in March, when I sought to reach Jim. His mother was very ill. We thought she was dying. I first reached out to Jim in meditation to be sure he knew of her illness; he seemed to be very near and aware. Then I made a request of him. Since I was doing a lot of traveling, I asked that he give me notice in advance, if that was possible for him to do, if his mother was going to die, so that I could be with her while she made the transition. I felt assured that he would do this, and I carried out my speaking engagements, trusting that I would know if I should *not* go. Such notification did not come to me during Mom's four months of serious illness, and she did not die.

His mother reported, during this time, almost daily visits with James, as she calls him. It seemed as though he kept "checking" on her to see how she was doing. She often complained to me that he was always in such a hurry. That he would come and visit for about an hour, and then he would have to rush off because he had so much to do. This was certainly typical of Jim as we knew him on this plane!

One day Mom was reporting to me her conversation with Jim from that morning. She said he had been with her most of the morning. It occurred to me to ask, "How did he look?"

"Well, to tell you the truth," she said, her full maternal tone coming into play, "he looked a little peaked."

On other occasions when Jim's mother has been ill, I

have felt Jim near and vigilant. Since Jim is her only child, I know that his link with her is strong, and I am sure he is very aware of major shifts in her Life Energy as they take place.

Just recently, Pearl became quite ill again. I was about to leave on an extended trip to the East, so I sat down to meditate, seeking clarity on how serious her condition was and whether I could go on or should stay. I had not had Jim on my mind at all. My intention was to focus in on Pearl herself, Higher Self to Higher Self.

Almost immediately, I found myself linked up with Jim instead. It was as though he was already near his mother, and thus when I zeroed in on her frequency, I got him. At once I knew he was still honoring my request that he let me know when his mother is about to die so I can be there. And this event took place over *five years* after I first asked that favor of him. Time as we know it seems to make no difference in relationships that transcend the physical body.

There have been many other meaningful moments of communication and sharing for me with Jim, many of which I share in the pages that follow. On the whole, these have taken place since I finished my grieving and began to build a new life on my own. I feel good about this, because our relationship here in the flesh was based on great strength in each of us. We came together as equal pillars sharing out of our fullness and lack of need, and thus doubly enriched our lives. So it has also been since his death. We have been sharing with each other as equals, exploring new terrain where we are and staying in touch with each other through the process. Never have I leaned on him, been dependent on him, or asked him to take responsibility for any aspect of my life. Nor have I felt him to be leaning on, or drawing on, me. For that I am grateful, and I affirm my path and his.

Sentimental Missing and Nostalgia

In February a new dimension of grieving emerged—a more superficial one, as I experienced it. I began missing Jim on a more day-to-day basis, noting his absence in the little things of life. Missing his touch, his laugh, his habits and patterns of relating, his jokes. The missing had moved to a more romantic and sentimental plane. I remembered more and more clearly what we had shared together and felt a nostalgia, a longing, for those personal sharings, knowing they would not be again—at least in this form.

Often these memories would take me completely by surprise. I remember one occasion when Scott and I were getting off an airplane at Kennedy Airport in New York. As we emerged from the passenger loading ramp into the waiting area, my glance took in the whole scene quickly. Instantly my mind matched that glance with a picture image of a time when Jim and I had arrived in that very same lobby area in New York. Just as instantly, a flood of tears began. There was no thought process in between. There was only the memory, and with it the pain of missing Jim and the accompanying release of that pain in tears. It was only when the whole transaction was finished that I was able to share with Scott what had happened.

Other times, the smell of shaving lotion like Jim's, or a voice that resembles his, or someone's walk or physique (especially from the back), or a gesture has triggered a memory so clear that in an instant I would be with Jim and in an instant he would be "gone." The cleansing rush of tears would again wash away my pain.

After *Search* came out, I did a number of television shows on which I shared the story of what had happened to us in Israel. The night I was on the David Frost Show, I was waiting just off stage for the final song of the guest who preceded me. She sang a love song that spoke of awaking in the morning to find her loved one was not there. The tears gushed forth as I remembered what seemed like a million such mornings, and I thought I might not be able to go on camera at all.

Such was my time of recovery. In the midst of ongoing

life, memories would unexpectedly surface, and I would be in the joy and pain of them, washing my inner being clear again with my tears. The pain lasted a shorter time and was more easily expressed the more often it happened. It seems there was a cumulative releasing of stored memories.

There were five days in late February when for the first time in the six months since Jim's death I was completely without any sense of grieving. There was tremendous relief in this, and I caught a glimpse of how it would be sometime in the future when I had really worked through the grief. These days of reprieve gave me confidence as I looked to the future.

Even though March and April brought a return of the heaviness of grieving, it was more low key and less acutely painful than before. A future-oriented serenity had settled in, and I began to develop a self-confidence that I *did* have something to contribute that would be important in the larger scheme of things, and that I *could* make that contribution even without Jim. Moreover, I felt that whatever I did, it would be an expression also of "us," of Jim and me together, giving our gift as two-in-one.

Energy-Draining Experiences

One of the most difficult periods during my months of recovery was the first month or two of my mother-in-law's severe illness. Pearl had a case of severe heart failure in the middle of March—something that did not surprise me, because she had suffered the loss of her only son. In fact, I was surprised that her strength held out as long as it did. She is a remarkable woman, and her strength and perseverance in the face of difficulty are not only admirable and unusual; they are also real indicators of the roots of those same qualities that came to fruition in Jim's life and personality.*

While Mom was ill—and especially during the early

* See *The Death and Life of Bishop Pike,* by William Stringfellow and Anthony Towne. New York: Doubleday, 1976.

weeks when we thought certain she was dying—I felt a tremendous energy drain in me. Partly it was from spending much time with Mom in the health care unit of the retirement residence where she lives. Giving to her, caring for her, talking with her. She seemed to be between two worlds most of the time and talked of preparing herself for death. I drew on Higher Self strength in these exchanges, but there was an emotional strain too.

Partly the drain was due to time and energy spent with Jim's Aunt Ethyl Larkey, who had come to be beside Pearl during her illness. Ethyl needed as much attention as Pearl did, for she was facing the impending loss of the last living member of her immediate family. I spent long hours listening to and talking with Ethyl. She was often nervous, distraught, exhausted, and fearful. Much of my physical and emotional strength was spent with her.

Third, I was still working a full schedule, doing a lot of speaking and traveling, radio and television interviews, and answering a great deal of mail. And there were growing numbers of persons who were coming to me with their own grief reactions to Jim's death, wanting to talk, looking for solace in my strength, sharing their pain.

Finally I began having fantasies of death taking all my loved ones, and my Little Self began fearing she could not survive another death, another loss. I especially feared the death of my own mother or father, or of Scott. My Little Self kept screaming she could not stand the pain of that. This "grief in anticipation" took a great emotional toll.

Perhaps these fantasies were the most draining of all, for they took me out of the reality I was living in—for which I have found there is *always* sufficient strength—and into a future that was nonexistent. My mind's projections of what *might* happen, and what my response *might* be, were ways of expending my energy uselessly at a time when I needed it all for the tasks at hand.

There were periods when I was so exhausted I thought I couldn't make it. I had no reserves of strength, and when mine was spent, it was really gone. At one point of exhaustion, I called and asked my mother to come and relieve me by staying with Ethyl and being with Pearl during the day so that I would have more time to myself. Having Mother with us for four or five days saved me temporarily. On another occasion when I hit bottom, I called my friend Patricia Bradley and asked her to come. I will never forget the impact of calling in the early morning to say "help" and returning from seeing Pearl at about 2 P.M. to find Patricia at my door to welcome me. Just seeing her there—"instant Patricia"—was like having an injection of strength and energy.

It is hard to describe how much it meant to me to have family and friends to count on during that time. But I am also aware that I, from my Higher Self, gave my Little Self the gift of calling for help when she needed it. Both the asking and the giving are of equal importance, for no one could have helped me if I had not been willing to receive. This is why *providing people with the opportunity to give* is such an important key to higher consciousness living.

Turning Toward the Future

Perhaps the most important aspect of the recovery was the series of future-oriented, meaning-giving experiences that came during this time. The first was the directive in Israel to return there for six months. Then, in February, I had an imaging session, while at a Spiritual Frontiers Fellowship Conference in Miami, Florida, in which I saw myself working in a "Center of Wholeness." I "saw" interpersonal and Higher Self–oriented work going on at many different levels, and I "saw" several friends of mine involved in the work with me. This was the first specific image to emerge of a future focus and form for my work and service.

A third was a sharing I had with my friend Laurel Keyes

from Denver. Laurel suggested that it might be helpful for me to be in touch with some of my past lives to see what specific tasks, or work, I had yet to do in this lifetime. She sat with me while I went into deep relaxation, and together we explored vivid memories that came out of what seemed to be my distant past. Those glimpses of my past incarnations provided me with a larger perspective on my present life and enabled me to begin to see deeper meaning in the events I was then living through.

Fourth, in May I read *The Autobiography of a Yogi* by Paramahansa Yogananda.* In the course of that reading, a whole new sense of direction and structure and vocation began to emerge. I sent for the series of correspondence lessons offered by the Self-Realization Fellowship that Yogananda founded, and launched into an intensive program of spiritual growth and development.

And fifth, on the weekend of the United States invasion of Cambodia, in May of 1970, I felt the first real surge of new emotional energy from within me. I had been active in the antiwar movement for six years—writing letters and sending telegrams to public officials, planning and taking part in educational programs about the war in Indochina, giving speeches about peace, and participating in peace vigils, fasts, and demonstrations. On the Cambodian invasion weekend, I found myself alone in our home in Santa Barbara without any ready-made outlet for my feelings of frustration about the war.

On Tuesday night of that week, I had given a talk to the League of Women Voters in Lompoc. At the end of the talk someone had said, "Have you ever thought of running for President of the United States?" I had not. But that woman's question lined up inside me along with many others that, over the months, had revealed to me what I saw as the great frustration of Americans in their eagerness to find someone—any-

* Published by the Self-Realization Fellowship, 3880 San Rafael Avenue, Los Angeles, Ca., 90065.

one—who would offer them an alternative to the political realities of the 1960's.

I spent a great deal of time that weekend dealing with my own frustrations in the same regard. I felt angry—bordering on violence—about the apparent unwillingness of our political leaders to listen and respond to the growing dissatisfaction of the "common people"—us voters and taxpayers—as we urged them to stop perpetrating violence in Southeast Asia.

Then it occurred to me that our government *could* declare war on Cambodia and even China, and then the Indochinese war would be not only legal but global. Since one of my main "arguments" against the war had been that it was illegal, I asked myself what I would do then. Moving to another country did not seem a helpful alternative, for, according to my values, all governments have their flaws. But I also knew I could in no way be a part of, or party to, a third World War.

I decided I would want to become a leader in an underground movement preparing for life *after* the war—a live alternative to destruction and death.

It was then I realized that I could offer *no* alternative as long as I was experiencing in me the same frustration, judgmentalism, criticism, hostility, distrust, and violence that led to wars to begin with. I could only offer an alternative to war when I had learned to *be* at peace in my own life.

The motivation from within was powerful. I wanted to *do* something—to *be* an alternative. My inner well of strength was reawakened, and I was infused with energy that I sought to channel into new and creative expression.

I decided I would eradicate all forms of violence, hostility, negativity, criticism, and frustration from my own being so that I could mirror peace in my own life. In that moment I touched on another important principle of higher consciousness living. I would *be the change I wanted to see happen*. I would *live* peace.

That weekend marked a major turning point in my journey through grief. It was like the reawakening of my inner well of strength—that strength I had drawn on before Jim's death, during our ordeal in the desert, and during the period of shock. Now my inner strength was again infusing me with energy that could be directed into something new and creative.

The rising tide of a whole new phase of my life experience had begun. As the water level of my Higher Self grew within me, it began to overtake the dry sands of grief and to bring life-giving water to my inner being. Out of these inner depths would arise the fruits of new growth. As pain was increasingly swallowed up in the swelling of Higher Self insight and understanding, purpose and direction, grief came to an end and I began to build my new life, to *create my own reality consciously,* just nine months after Jim's death.

7

BUILDING A NEW LIFE
A New Birth

To say that grief ended nine months after Jim's death is true in only one sense: I turned my attention away from the past and toward the future after that time. I was finished with my grief for what I had "lost" and began to look forward to what lay ahead.

There is another sense in which the handling of my grief continued: I was still having periods of deep pain as late as three years later; I was making major adjustments to the fact of my being a "widow" into my fifth year after Jim's death, and as I have been writing this manuscript in the sixth year, pain has been reawakened over and over again.

When I think of persons who have lost their mates after forty, fifty, or sixty years of a totally shared life, I am no longer surprised that some of them do not ever manage to finish grief and get on with building a new life. It seems to me that once we have suffered the death of a very dear one, grief never ceases completely. Because that person was so very important to our lives at one point, he remains important forever.

What we deal with, then, are degrees and shadings of the experience we call grief—and especially of suffering and recovery. We each have our own pattern of timing, but even when the most intense grief is over, we continue to uncover new layers of pain as we build and live out our new life.

The Question of Remarriage

Almost from the time of Jim's death, people began to ask me if I would remarry. Some were curious about whether my conviction that Jim was still alive in spite of the death of his body would make me feel I couldn't marry another because I was still married to Jim.

For four years, the only answer I could give to that question was "I don't know." I certainly did not feel inhibited by my relationship with Jim. We had talked before his death about the fact that both of us would want the other to remarry if the other were to die. We had not had feelings of exclusion about our relationship while Jim was alive, so I certainly didn't feel any after his death. Hence I was open to the possibility of remarriage, but I wanted my future to unfold organically, from the inside out. I did not want to cling to any preconceived ideas about a "good life," for I did not yet know what magnificent surprises might lie ahead for me. This is the wisdom of *having no expectations but rather abundant expectancy* in the living of life.

I could never, for example, have conjured up in my imagination the life events that unfolded for me after meeting Jim. Our entire relationship, in life and in death, was completely different from any experiences I had had prior to that summer of 1966 when I met him. I stood in amazement and wonder at what life had held in store for me then; certainly I wanted to remain open to whatever was to come to me in the future.

Secondly, there was a sense in which I felt that it would be greedy of me to ask for or seek a new marriage. I knew that many people did not have in thirty or forty years of married life, or in three or four or five different marriages, the depth of sharing and total fulfillment I had known with Jim. I felt blessed to have had such a union at all. To ask for another seemed to border on excess.

I knew I would never meet another person like Jim. He was uniquely himself. I also knew I would never have another relationship like ours. It was uniquely what it was. Therefore, I was in no sense looking for a "replacement" for what Jim and I had known and shared. I chose to go forth instead with *no expectations at all* of what would bring me happiness or fulfillment in the future.

I felt secure living alone. I felt whole. There were no deep longings or unmet needs in me that I sought to have filled by another person. I felt my greatest opportunity lay in the realm of spiritual unfoldment and inner development, and it was to that that I turned my attention with new intensity.

My Spiritual Path

Only six months before I met Jim, I had had a series of life-changing experiences in which I had broken through to cosmic consciousness. I had experienced myself as one with All That Is, as an essential part of the universe, as one expression of the Whole. In these events, I came to know myself as whole and integral, rather than as divided against myself. I knew my Oneness with all other persons, and I knew that the Life Force that filled me and all human beings was indestructible and all-encompassing.

When I met Jim, I had the great privilege of sharing all these knowings with another person. In our marriage union, I lived out my sense of Oneness with the All through an experience of total Oneness with another.

Now I felt I had the opportunity to move on. Grief had been a cleansing for me. I had been letting go of all the bonds that tied me physically, emotionally, and mentally to Jim in order to enjoy a new kind of union with him and with all others. Having my loved one pass through the threshold of death so that any relationship we now had, transcended, of necessity, the physical limitations of time and space, was to have an open door to the potential of universal loving and relating in all areas of my life. I wanted to develop that potential by moving on to other forms of loving.

There was still more cleansing to undergo. If I was to live in total peace and harmony with all persons everywhere, I had to eradicate from my life all hostilities, resentments, criticisms, and expressions of negativity of whatever kind, whether or not I was choosing to manifest them.

I looked forward to my six months in Israel as a time to undergo that cleansing. I would be out of my familiar environment, away from the negative vibrations of frustration and anger that permeated so much of our society that year (1970), as I experienced it, and into the writing of the book on the historical Jesus in Israel. Surely the setting would be right for a renewal and rejuvenation of my spirit.

My brother and I spent the summer of 1970 doing extensive research for the writing of the book that Jim had left unfinished. We had shared in Jim's research and preparation for the book since 1968, and we knew Jim had felt it would be his most important contribution to the field of Biblical scholarship and theology. We had determined, therefore, to finish the project after Jim's death as our gift and tribute to him—a "memorial" of a very special kind.

There was a sense, then, in which the writing of *The Wilderness Revolt** was a part of our grief work, for we really did it *for* Jim, and he was much in our conscious awareness all during the process of writing.

By September, we had organized ourselves sufficiently to move our writing project to Israel. All the plans had worked out beautifully to enable us to go—a clear indication, for me, that it was in harmony with the larger plan for our lives. I had

* By Diane Kennedy Pike and R. Scott Kennedy, New York: Doubleday & Co., 1972.

found a companion to live with Jim's mother; a priest-friend was coming to live in my house and manage the Foundation while I was gone; royalty payments on *The Other Side** enabled me to afford the cost of our six-month stay; and Scott had arranged his college credits so that he could complete his fall quarter of schooling while in Israel.

We arrived in Israel just one year to the week from the time of the search for Jim in the desert, and Scott and I were able to visit St. Peter's Protestant Cemetery in Jaffa on the first anniversary of the committal service.

Cleansing Myself of Fear

Immediately upon arrival, I became aware that there were still things for me to work out with the land, Israel. Fears still lurked inside me that death would strike again while we were there, this time taking Scott and leaving me bereft once again.

I determined to face it all—driving a rented car on back roads, letting Scott "go," traveling alone in that "foreign" land, and even returning to the canyon where Jim and I had struggled against death and Jim had made his transition.

Scott and I spent our first two and a half months studying Hebrew at the University in Jerusalem. We worked on the book as well, but we felt that some knowledge of Hebrew would be helpful to us in relating to modern-day Israelis as well as in comprehending the mentality of Jesus.

Then we rented a car and took off for two weeks of sightseeing in the north, the region of Galilee. We stayed at the Italian Hospice on the Mount of Beatitudes, traveling some days and writing on others. We went into remote areas we had never visited, seeing all the sites of any possible historical significance.

There were several opportunities for me to deal with my

* By James A. Pike with Diane Kennedy, New York: Doubleday & Co., 1968.

fear of driving in unknown territory. Scott and I took many side trips onto little-traveled roads in order to visit ruins of crusader castles and key sites in the history of Israel. When the road would get rough, or would be much longer than we had thought, panic would begin to set in. In each case I dealt directly with my Little Self feelings. Scott and I talked about them; from my Higher Self I encouraged Little Self to feel the fear and experience the energy of it; then I urged my mind to observe all the elements of those experiences that were like the one with Jim, and all that were very different, so that patterns of association which had begun to crystallize could be quickly broken down.

At the end of the two weeks, Scott left to spend a month on a kibbutz in the Negev. I drove him to the bus station in Tel Aviv, and as I returned to Galilee alone, I began to be almost sick with anxiety. It took several days for me to identify what was going on. Then I realized I was listening to news broadcasts and reading the papers daily with an almost unconscious expectation that I would read of an accident of some kind in which an American named Scott Kennedy had been killed.

Once I became aware of my fear, I practiced releasing Scott daily to his own perfect pattern, or into "God's hands." Before the end of two weeks, that fear for Scott's life, and my potential "loss," had also been purged.

The major cleansing with regard to fears linked to the past experience with Jim came on the last day of Scott's and my stay in Israel. Another group of our friends and members of the Bishop Pike Foundation had come to Israel for a two-week trip. Among them were John and Ellen Downing. Just before returning to the States, Scott and I made arrangements to go out into the desert, retracing the steps Jim and I had taken. An Israeli friend who is an experienced guide went with us, as did John and Ellen and two other Americans with whom we had become friends while in Israel.

We drove to the mouth of the canyon where Jim and I had begun the hardest part of our walk, and then hiked into the canyon. I dealt with anxiety and panic the whole way—especially when Scott would get so far ahead of us that we would lose sight of him. When at last we reached the place where Jim fell and died, however, a strange sense of peace came over me. We stayed there a long time—John, Ellen, Scott, and I—weeping for our loss of Jim and rejoicing in the continuity of the events and relationships of our lives. It was a privilege for the four of us to be able to return there together and to share Jim's final hours on earth with him, if only in imagination, a whole year and a half later.

A Gravestone for Jim

The time in Israel also afforded me an opportunity to have a marker prepared for the gravesite in Jaffa. I had inquired about a marker at the time of the burial, but as it is the custom in Israel to place a stone over the grave itself, as well as to have an upright marker if that is desired, I was informed the stone could not be erected until at least a year had passed, so that the ground would be fully settled.

Scott and I selected a rough-hewn Jerusalem stone and had it polished on only one side so that it would suggest the rocks on which Jim had climbed and fallen and on which he had died. We had the marker inscribed: "James A. Pike, Bishop (P.E.C.U.S.A.) ✠ Born 1913, Oklahoma City, Okla., Died 1969, Judean Wilderness." On the gravestone itself we put: "We have this treasure in earthen vessels, to show that the transcendent power belongs to God and not to us" (II Cor. 4:7) and "And Life Is Victorious!" (Mandaean Book of Prayer)—two favorite citations of Jim's which seemed singularly appropriate for his gravestone.

The stone was actually erected in November of 1970, but we did not dedicate it until February, when the tour group arrived from the States. Since John Downing had officiated at the committal service, it seemed fitting that he and I should also plan and preside over the dedication of the stone. In pouring rain on a bleak February morning in 1971, then, nineteen friends of Jim's gathered for prayers and tributes in quiet little St. Peter's Cemetery in Jaffa.

Thus there were many ways in which I was tying up the loose ends of grief during the thirteenth to the eighteenth months after Jim's death. Scott and I worked steadily for well over six months—and almost ten hours a day for over two and a half months in Israel—to complete the manuscript that put forward Jim's thesis on the historical life of Jesus. It was with a great feeling of triumph that we mailed it off to our publisher at the end of January 1971, with copies going to three leading scholars who had promised to give us their straightforward criticism and suggestions.

The Plunge Deeper

Of equal importance to the "finishing up" was the new life-thrust I was making for myself. Only a short while after we got settled in Israel, I received an "ultimatum" during my regular meditation one morning. It was *Either you plunge deeper, or die.* My sense was that if I were to "stand still," spiritually, at that juncture in my life, it would be the same as moving backward, or "dying."

So I made a new level of commitment to my spiritual life and growth. I was ready to go deeper and to do whatever was necessary toward that end.

I began rising at 4:30 A.M. with the Muslim call to prayer and spending two and a half hours in prayer, meditation, exercises, and study before going down to breakfast in the small hotel where Scott and I were living. This seemed to be an important new beginning. Then at the end of a two-week stay alone at the Scottish Hospice in Tiberias, a most important next step was shown to me.

I awoke one Friday morning with a tremendous sense that something important was about to happen to me. I didn't know what, but the sense was so strong that I left a letter to a friend open so I could write her about it after it happened! I had planned a boat trip across the Sea of Galilee that morning. I thought, *Perhaps that will be the time.*

I sat down to have my lunch at Kibbutz Ein Gev, across the lake. Their specialty is Peter Fish out of the Sea of Galilee, and as the waitress set my plate before me, I looked down into the eye of the fish and suddenly felt sick to my stomach. *To think that only a short time ago that fish was alive and well, swimming in the lake, and now I am about to eat its flesh.*

I had never before thought of fish as having flesh. My mind marshaled all its reasoning forces to convince my Little Self that it was really all right to eat the fish, but the phrase "eat its flesh" kept coming back into my awareness over and over again, and in the end I left the fish almost untouched.

I took the boat back to Tiberias right after lunch, thinking to myself, *Well, it didn't happen.* I determined to go back to my room and finish typing the chapter I was working on. When I discovered I was almost out of typing paper, I quickly sealed the letter to my friend, grabbed my wallet, and rushed out to the store.

It was Friday afternoon, and I knew that most of the store owners closed their shops early in order to be home in plenty of time for the beginning of Sabbath at sunset. As I rushed past the Hospice office, I heard someone typing. I stuck my head in the door and said to the woman there, "Excuse me. Could you please tell me where I could buy some typing paper here in Tiberias?" I thought perhaps she could save me the time of looking and asking.

"Nowhere at this hour," she replied.

In great surprise I said, "But it's only two P.M."

"I know," she said politely, "but the stores close early for the Sabbath here in Tiberias."

"Thank you," I responded, drawing my head back out of the door. I heaved a sigh of resignation and decided to go mail the letter anyway.

As I returned from the post office, I heard the typewriter clacking steadily away. Feeling I had been a bit abrupt before, I stepped in and said, "I'm sorry to have been so brusque. I do thank you for the information."

The woman looked up from her typewriter. I had met her briefly before when I had come to select a room to stay in at the Hospice. She had a lovely, bright face with cheeks glowing in health. Her white hair was pulled back in a tidy bun, and her eyes danced with life. Suddenly she was up on her feet, rummaging in a small satchel that rested on a chair beside her desk.

"Do you need much paper?" she was asking. I told her of the chapter I was finishing. "Well, then perhaps you could use some of this." She handed me some typing paper—precisely the kind I had been using. "It isn't fancy," she was saying, "but it's what I use."

She was back to her typewriter again, and I stood in the center of the room, feeling rather awkward and overwhelmed. I thanked her profusely for her generosity, and then, wanting somehow to make up for having burst in on her like that and *not* wanting just to walk off with her gift, I said, "What are *you* working on?"

"It's a booklet on healing," she said softly.

A *Challenge for Me*

Something jarred inside me. I made a comment or asked another question, and soon we were into a conversation. I began sharing with her my concern about the war in Vietnam and how I had come to Israel hoping to eradicate from my being all negativity, hostility, violence, and criticism so that I could be a living example of peace at work in at least one life. The woman, whose name I still did not know, looked at me directly and said, "Let me put a challenge to you."

Time stood still for just a moment. Inside me I knew that whatever she was about to say was not only *for me*, it was the reason for my having come to Israel in the first place. That directive to spend six months in Israel, received eleven months earlier, in January, had pointed to this moment. Here was my specific opportunity to "plunge deeper," spiritually. Before she spoke again, I knew I would say "yes" to her challenge.

"I am convinced," she said earnestly, "that until we stop devouring the flesh of our brother and sister creatures, and until we stop shedding their blood to meet our own selfish desires, we will not be able to stop killing one another."

That fish flashed before my mind's eye, and I heard the words "eat its flesh." The experience at lunch had been in preparation for this moment.

She went on, speaking of the Holy, Harmless Way of Life and of the Kingdom of Heaven on earth, and soon she was handing me a booklet to read on the subject. Her name was on the cover: she was Miss Hannah Hurnard. I thanked her and left.

On my way to my room, I felt a new bounce in my step. Something was happening. Something was *really* going on. A young man—very obviously American—sat waiting on a bench outside the dining room. For a moment I thought he was waiting for me. Then I realized that was ridiculous, so I bounded on up the stairs to get washed for dinner. As it turned out, my thought had not been so ridiculous at all.

I had been eating my meals each evening with members of the United Nations Observers' Corps, but that evening none of them came, and I was alone at my table for the first time in two weeks. Soon Hannah came in with the young American and sat down at the table next to me. I couldn't help but overhear their words and their talk of the work of the Spirit in their lives.

A prompting from my Higher Self said, *Go join them.* Before my mind could list all the reasons why I shouldn't, I got up, took my plate, and said, "May I join you?"

Walking in the Light

The rest of the weekend was filled with intermittent sharings with Hannah and the young American, Paul Buser. I was caught up in the energy of the "perfect pattern" again. Paul had come all the way from California to meet Hannah, and so had I, without knowing it. He and I had much to share, and I found the inner movement in me so rapid as to almost leave me breathless.

At the end of my morning meditation on Saturday I decided to give up meat-eating as a symbol of my desire to be cleansed of all negativity, and I moved forward in my inner being to meet the "more" that was yet to come.

All during my deepest grieving I had carried a metaphorical image in my mind: I was standing on the threshold of an open doorway; before me there was nothing but Light. I knew the threshold was grief, and I felt that when I stepped through the door, that is, when I had finished grief, a way would become clear before me and I would know which direction to go.

On Sunday afternoon I went for a walk alone by the Sea of Galilee. Suddenly I realized I was walking in the Light. I was no longer on the threshold; the door itself was behind me and I was in the Light!

Then a great realization came to me. I heard in my inner ear the message Jesus had preached when he launched his public work in Galilee: "the Kingdom of God is at hand; repent and follow me." Suddenly I "saw" what he meant. There was no "way" to look for in that Light beyond my threshold. The way *was* the Light; the Light *was* the Way. The Kingdom of God was already here, around me, within me. If I wanted to live in it, all I had to do was change the way I was living (repent) and "follow Jesus"—that is, live as Jesus lived, the Kingdom-of-God way of life. Jesus had said, "I am the light of the world; he who follows me will not walk in darkness, but will have the light of life."

This *was* the way—to walk in the Light. That's all there was to it. I sang out in joy for the simplicity of it, and I announced aloud for all the world to hear: "From this day forth, I will walk in the Light and live the Kingdom-of-Heaven way of life. I will live as Jesus lived and walk as Jesus walked. Thanks be to God!"

The remainder of my time in Israel was filled with joyful cleansing. Each morning I stood in the Light and asked to be shown what else needed to be let go from my life, and what else I needed to do to restore harmony to my relationships with all persons. One directive after another came in loud and clear. I wrote letters to some persons against whom I had harbored resentments for years. I asked forgiveness for wrongs I had done. I reached out to persons I had neglected. I released all feelings of negativity and practiced perceiving the beauty in all persons I saw, especially those with whom I had previously found fault. I lived in a perpetual state of thanksgiving and joy, and my spirits soared to incredible new heights.

Meanwhile, completely without my knowing, a parallel breakthrough to a new and transformed way of living was taking place in the life of one Arleen Lorrance in Brooklyn, New York. Our paths did not cross until a year later, but already they were being brought into harmony through the choices we were making to live uncompromising lives of Light and Love.

Symbols of the New Me

I spent the months of January and February practicing living fully in my new state of being. I felt so completely "new" that I wanted to symbolize the change somehow. I decided I would no longer wear my wedding rings on my left hand. It seemed to me that to leave my ring finger bare was to say symbolically, "I now acknowledge that my marriage to Jim is ended in the form it once took. I am a single person again—whole and single."

The first day I went without the rings, I felt bereft. I

157

tried wearing them around my neck on a chain for a day or two; that also felt wrong. Several times I slipped them back on my left hand and lived in the comfort and ease of familiarity for a time. But I was determined to make the adjustment to not wearing the rings before I returned to the States.

Finally, I decided to wear the rings, mine and Jim's, on my right hand. They would still be with me, but no longer symbolizing a marriage in the terms our society acknowledges. I did not want to be seen as Jim's widow anymore. I wanted, instead, to be fully the new person I was becoming.

8

BUILDING A NEW LIFE
Finding My Own Way

I REMEMBER the first time someone referred to me as "Bishop Pike's widow." The term "widow" struck me as harsh, even cruel. Partly there was the finality of it, partly, the nonidentity I felt in it.

I was a person—a person who had chosen to share my life with a man named Jim Pike. I had been myself, first—a complete, whole, and competent person. Then I had become Jim's wife, and that had been a dynamic, life-giving, life-affirming relationship. Now I was a new "me"—a me without Jim beside me. But to be Jim's "widow" felt restrictive—like having identity only in relation to what once was, to be wedded to the past.

While I was grieving, I didn't wrestle with the matter of my being Jim's widow. I had no energy for that, no interest in it. I accepted the designation as society's way of classifying me, and let it go at that. As I made my recovery from grief, however, and began to build my new life, the matter of my identity loomed larger and larger.

A Public Nonentity

When I returned from Israel, I began receiving invitations to give lectures and to be interviewed on TV shows, by magazines, etc. I had made many public appearances during the first nine months after Jim's death. I enjoyed lecturing and being interviewed. I felt confident in my abilities and at ease in the role. I had been surprised, however, that "the public" had sustained an interest in me. After all, it was Jim who had been famous, controversial, and a popular spokesman—not I.

Now I began to look again at the interest "the public" had in me and felt it to be primarily vicarious. That is, I began to feel that many persons had transferred to me their interest in and admiration for, and even anger at, Jim. It was as if I served as a vehicle through which they could continue to relate to Jim, even if only at a distance. I was the most tangible symbol of his ongoing influence in their lives, and they sought to be near him by meeting, touching, hearing me. And it was no wonder that that was their response, for I was always billed as "Widow of Bishop Pike." Sometimes my name was also mentioned—if the sign or poster had room for details.

I think of one particularly vivid experience. I had been invited to speak at a small junior college in Southern California, in the heart of political conservatism. Though my talk had been scheduled ahead of time as part of an ongoing series of lectures, it happened to fall on a date that the Vietnam Moratorium Committee selected as a day of protest against the war.

The dean of students informed me, as we drove from the airport to the campus, that there would be antiwar demonstrators out in front of the building where I would speak, but he hoped there would be no trouble.

I had chosen "Peace Begins Within" as my topic, and I spoke on my recent experiences of cleansing, which were the result of my decision to eradicate all forms of violence, negativity, and hostility from my own being. I shared my conviction that unless I lived at peace within my own being and with all persons I met, I could in no way make a contribution to peace in the society and world around me.

My talk really amounted to a "testimonial" out of my own experience. I did not argue any political issues related to the war in Vietnam. I was *being the change I wanted to see happen* by seeking to establish a harmonious relationship with *all* in attendance, whether or not we held the same political views.

When I finished and invited questions, one person after another stood up to lambast me as an anti-American and a radical. I was stunned by the anger I seemed to have aroused in them by my talk on peace—and *inner* peace at that! Finally a gentleman in the back invited all those who were loyal Americans to stand and give the pledge of allegiance to the flag. Then he stomped out of the gymnasium indignantly. A young demonstrator who had been seated at the back shouted, "Heil, Hitler!" and followed him out in goose-step formation.

Bewildered and somewhat overwhelmed by what had happened, I had responded to each of those who had shouted at me, remaining centered in my own sense of peace. At the end of the evening, many persons came forward to affirm, personally and on a one-to-one basis, their solidarity with my message. Then I left with the dean of students.

He apologized for the scene that had been created, saying that there were many people in that area who made an avocation of going to hear speakers they felt to be liberals or radicals, just to voice their dissent. "Your husband was such an outspoken critic of the war," he explained, "I'm sure they came armed to argue against you."

There it was—the mixing of my identity with Jim's. Had he said that they had come because *I* had been such an outspoken critic of the war, which I had, it would have been different. But no. It was against *Jim* that they were prepared to argue, and that is why they came to hear *me!*

The same thing happened over and over again with interviews. The reporter or host would say, "We would like to interview you, Mrs. Pike." Then all the questions would begin with, "What did your husband believe about . . ." or "Could you relate to us your husband's experiences with. . . ."

I began to feel nonexistent. It was as though Jim, by dying, had caused *me* to cease to be while living on himself.

I am sure every widow must go through such an identity crisis to one degree or another—and perhaps some widowers, too. Each of us is well known in our own circle of friends, and the struggle to be known for who we are, and not for who our husband was, must be a common one. That my struggle happened to be set in a larger arena because my husband was a well-known public figure did not alter the nature of the conflict.

I began to see that I had to make some clear choices and decisions if I did not wish to become a "professional widow." Some women choose that role. They *want* to continue to be identified as their husband's representative long years after his death. I did not want to. I wanted to go on living my own life, as I had both before I met Jim and while I knew and lived with him.

My first major decision, then, was to stop giving public lectures and doing interviews for the media. In the spring of 1971, I adopted a blanket rule for myself: I would turn down any and all future invitations to appear in public, no matter from whom they came or for what occasion. This decision lasted for over six months and temporarily relieved some of the pressure of the identity crisis.

The Larger Picture Emerges

Parallel with my growing identity crisis over being Jim's widow, my new sense of identity was emerging.

Upon my return from Israel in the winter of 1970, I

shared with a large group of friends in Santa Barbara—most of whom were members of The Bishop Pike Foundation—the cleansing I had undergone in my six months away. I told them of my decision to eradicate all violence, negativity, and hostility from my life in order to be able to live in peace. The idea emerged of forming a Peacemakers group, and several persons expressed interest in being part of it.

I viewed this as a possible indication of a new direction for the Foundation's program, which was still in a state of limbo. So I organized meetings of Foundation members in the Los Angeles and San Francisco areas to explore how much interest there would be in forming small groups, or "communities." Although the meetings were well attended, nothing really emerged in terms of clear interest or direction.

Then one morning in meditation, the thought came to me: *You have finished your three karmic tasks.* I was familiar, superficially, with the concept of karma, but I had never thought in terms of "karmic tasks." Therefore I was startled and puzzled by the thought.

That's nice, I thought. Then I asked in my inner being, *What were they?*

Immediately the answer came: *To learn that God and the Church are not one and the same, to learn the true meaning of chastity, and to learn to love [Jim] perfectly.*

I was absorbing the impact of this clear message from my own Higher Self, when the further thought came: *Now you can move on to your new mission for this life if you wish.*

I recorded the insights in my log. My Higher Self had "spoken" to me in concepts that were unfamiliar to me, and yet somehow it all made sense. I knew that these learnings were only for me, at my stage of development, and not necessarily universal truths. The meaning of chastity I had come to was true *for me*; the way I learned to love in my relationship with Jim was perfect *for me*. These same learnings could be quite different for someone else.

As I reflected on these insights over the next several

months, the larger picture of my life became clearer and clearer. I saw the interrelatedness between the various events and decisions of my life. It seemed that all my early years had been absorbed in my dedication to God *through the Church*. I had felt I could not serve God totally *outside* the Church, and that was one reason I had not wanted to marry a man who was not as dedicated to God and the Church as I was.

Then I met Jim. His depth of commitment matched mine, but he had already begun to distinguish between his covenant with God and his loyalty to the institutionalized expression of that—namely, the Church. He had begun to question all manifestations of idolatry—whether through worship of creed, code, or cult.*

In my three short years of knowing Jim, the threads of *my* life had been pulled taut. I learned to discriminate between the Church, as institution, and God, as the dynamic Life Force of the universe; I came to see and experience chastity as purity of the heart, or intention, rather than abstention from sexual activity per se; and I had loved fully, completely, and perfectly, in terms of my own ability to love, in my relationship with Jim.

Our experience in the Wilderness of Judea and Jim's death there had been a severe test of my learnings. I had been sustained by the Life Force, by God, in all aspects of that week-long search, and *not* solely through institutional expressions of His ministry and presence; I knew my first loyalty was to God even in the face of the death of my loved one, Jim, thus keeping my priorities straight and my heart pure; and I had loved Jim enough to *leave* him in order to find help for him, even though I would have preferred to die there with him. All these experiences had been like final tests to see if I had indeed learned my lessons well. Since I had, I could now move on if I was willing.

* See A *Time for Christian Candor*, by James A. Pike, New York: Harper & Row, 1964.

The New "Mission"

I had already committed myself to the new, but I knew that my time in Israel had been only a preparation for what was to come. I felt that there was so much more for me to learn and understand before I could begin to make a real contribution to others. Nevertheless, it was not long before I received a directive one morning: *You will begin to teach what you know.*

My Little Self trembled. *I'm not ready*, she protested to my Higher Self. *I'm not strong enough to do what you are asking.*

Unless you begin to share what you have already received, you will not be given more, came the response.

As I understand the thoughts and insights that come to me from my Higher Self, they are what many call the "still, small voice within." The Higher Self is my individualized expression of the Universal Mind, or God. It is my direct contact with the perfect pattern for my life, or "God's Will." The thoughts come to me when I am still within, when I ask, and when I am willing to recognize, to receive, and to act on them.

In this case I said, *All right*, I [Little Self] *am willing if you* [Higher Self] *will show me the way.*

That very afternoon I went down to the Downings' to meet some friends of theirs. Other Santa Barbara friends had also been invited, and in the course of conversation, completely out of any relevant context, one of them, Jackie, said, "Well, Diane, when are you going to organize our Peacemakers study group?"

Several months had passed since any of us had mentioned a Peacemakers group, and never had we said it would be a study group. I looked at Jackie with wide eyes. Then I shared my inner "directive" of that morning, and soon we had set a date for the first meeting of the Peacemakers.

We had about twelve sessions that summer, and I received all the material for each class session through my morning meditations. My Higher Self had taken over because my Little Self was willing to be guided. Most of the material from these classes has since been incorporated into a little book called *Channeling Love Energy,** self-growth handbook for persons who want to live in love and peace.

In those class sessions, I was being fully myself—my *new* self. The persons who came wanted to study with me because of what I had to offer, not because of who Jim had been. I reached into the center of my own being, and gave all that I discovered there freely, with no reluctance to share the new insights that came. I was beginning to do something new: to give fully of myself from my own center of inner knowing, with my own life experience as the textbook out of which I gained my learning.

The First Break from the Past

That same summer (1971, almost two years after Jim's death), I received a second directive from my Higher Self. It was to sell our house in Santa Barbara and move to Denver, where I would open a center for spiritual growth and study, in cooperation with Laurel Keyes.

Laurel was a friend who had come into my life just one month before Jim's death. During grief and in the period of recovery which followed, she was instrumental in putting me in touch with "ancient wisdom"—a noninstitutionalized tradition of teaching spiritual truths which dates back to the Egyptians, if not earlier than that. Since I was learning a new way to walk in the Light, my association with Laurel had been uplifting and broadening. I felt she had been given me as a gift to help see me through the transition that grief represented.

Twice I had gone to Denver to spend time at the retreat

* By Diane K. Pike and Arleen Lorrance, LP Publications, P.O. Box 7601, San Diego, Ca. 92107, 1976.

site that belonged to Laurel and the group she helped form, called the Fransisters and Franbrothers. It was that retreat to which I was directed by my Higher Self, and with Laurel's full and joyful participation, I began laying plans to leave California and move to Colorado.

I had often been asked since Jim's death whether I would stay in Santa Barbara. My answer had been: "Until and unless I have some reason to move elsewhere." Now I had a reason. I determined I would go if doors opened easily for me, and I thus felt assured that the move was in harmony with my perfect pattern.

Everything fell into place quickly. Our house sold within a week after I put it on the market and before the real estate agents had even put it on their lists. Jim's Aunt Ethyl Larkey decided to move to Santa Barbara to live with his mother, Pearl Chambers, so neither of them would be alone. Gertrude Platt, my secretary and good friend, had a son who lived in Littleton, the suburb of Denver I was moving to, and she agreed to go along to help me establish an office there. She and her husband had been planning to visit their children there anyway. And so it went.

Thus I made definite plans to leave Santa Barbara and the home Jim and I had shared. I felt strong enough, in my Little Self, to take that step, but I also recognized it as my first real move away from the past that I had shared fully with Jim and into my new life. It was a major change, and I did not make it lightly.

My Face in Spiritual Paintings

One other important part of the larger picture began to come into focus that same summer. My close friend Patricia Bradley had gone to San Diego to take part in a three-week workshop at the National Center for the Exploration of Human Potential. She met there one Arleen Lorrance, who had been brought to California on a scholarship because of her initiation of THE LOVE PROJECT at a ghetto high school in Brooklyn, New York.*

Arleen had invited Patricia to her apartment to see her spiritual paintings, and Patricia had had a strong feeling that *I* had to see those paintings as well. When she told me so, I agreed I would be glad to meet Arleen when (if ever) I was next in San Diego.

That seemed like a safe approach, since I had been to San Diego only twice in my life and it didn't seem likely I would be there again soon. I had very little interest in seeing someone's "spiritual paintings," even though I had high regard for Patricia's intuition. Ever since Jim's death, I had been deluged with sharings from people of their psychic messages, photographs, and other experiences. I was really saturated and could have done without this latest variation on what I assumed would be the same theme. My *expectations* had temporarily blotted out my *abundant expectancy* in the realm of the "spiritual."

The very next week I received a call from Doubleday asking me to go to San Diego to speak to their West Coast salesmen about *The Wilderness Revolt*. I agreed to do it and felt the invitation to be directly connected to Patricia's strong feeling that I should meet Arleen Lorrance. This was an example of one of those open doors that characterize the unfolding of the perfect pattern.

I found Arleen to be a dynamic, outgoing, energetic person whose enthusiasm was almost overwhelming. From the moment we said hello until I left to go to the airport, Arleen talked almost nonstop, pouring out her story, of which the paintings were an integral part.

She told me of her spiritual awakening in the fall of 1969 and of beginning to paint paintings that "paint themselves." She said she often had a plan in mind when she began, but

* For the full story, read *The Love Project*, by Arleen Lorrance, LP Publications, P.O. Box 7601, San Diego, Ca. 92107, 1972.

that she allowed the brushes to "do their own thing" in her hands. The result was that faces appeared on the canvas which she had not consciously put there.

Arleen showed me the first of a series of paintings and said, "Do you see the woman's face at the bottom of the painting?" I didn't, but immediately I had the overwhelming sense that *I* was the woman in her painting. I didn't say anything, however, because I felt it would be presumptuous of me. After all, I had only just met Arleen.

As we went from painting to painting and the woman's face became clearer and clearer, I was more and more certain that I was she. Arleen had been showing me that face in particular because it kept recurring in her paintings, and she had not been able to discover who the woman was.

The hour and a half sped by. I had to leave. Arleen said she felt we had more to explore together. I invited her to come to Santa Barbara for the weekend in two weeks. She agreed, and I left.

When I got on the airplane, I almost immediately fell into a very deep sleep. The next thing I knew, there were two persons calling to me. I felt as though I were pulling myself up out of a deep, dark well. Only with great effort did I finally bring the stewardess's face into focus. She was saying something to me, but I could not sort out the words. I didn't remember where I was or what was happening.

After what felt like eons, I realized I was on an airplane and we were about to land in Los Angeles. Twenty minutes had passed since we left San Diego. The stewardess wanted me to bring my seat to an upright position for the landing.

I don't remember ever having been in a deeper sleep. It was as though I had gone into the deep recesses of my own being as a response to the sharing with Arleen. I had left myself wide open to her, and something profound was happening in me as a result.

Two weeks later, Arleen and her husband, Dick, came to

Santa Barbara for the weekend. As I was making a salad for dinner on Friday evening, I said, "Arleen, I didn't say this to you in San Diego, because I thought it would sound presumptuous, but I'm the woman in your paintings."

Arleen shrieked with delight. As we compared stories, we realized that we had had that awareness at the same moment —while Arleen was showing me the first painting. She hadn't said anything either, because she had felt it would be presumptuous! We decided to eliminate that word from our vocabulary from then on!

The rest of the weekend was filled with joyful explorations of Santa Barbara, interspersed with deeply meaningful sharings. Arleen told me at length about THE LOVE PROJECT— a way she had found to be open, loving, and vulnerable all the time while teaching in a ghetto high school in Brooklyn. The more we shared, the more deeply connected with one another we felt at a nonverbal level.

A Mirror to Look In

Two weeks later, at the end of October, I left Santa Barbara. I had plenty of help getting packed. Friends volunteered, Scott was there, and my mother came down from San Jose for several days to lend a hand. As paintings came off the walls and books down from the shelves, I felt as though I was dismantling Jim's and my relationship. All that was left by way of a physical manifestation of our life together—the house, a kind of "outer shell" of our marriage, which had been of such comfort to my Little Self during grief—was being disassembled, item by item. I found myself grieving again, not with deep pain but with sadness and wistfulness for what once was and was no more.

I settled in comfortably to the little cabin at the retreat site in the mountains near Denver where I was to live. Weeks sped by as we laid the groundwork for the center we would open. Plans moved ahead unimpeded.

For Christmas I asked the Father, God, for a gift. I wanted a glimpse of my "perfection" so that I could bring myself into harmony with it. As is the Father's way, the gift began coming around Thanksgiving and was completed in January on my thirty-fourth birthday. It came in four parts, all of which were deeply meaningful insights and experiences. I share only one here because of its direct relevance to the unfolding of the larger picture of my life.

After a Bishop Pike Foundation meeting in Santa Barbara on New Year's Day, I went to San Diego to visit Arleen and Dick for a few days. Arleen had shared with me that she had a deep feeling there was some work we were to do together. We explored the possibilities before us and made plans for her to visit me in Denver. Then one afternoon we went for a walk out on the pier in Ocean Beach, the section of San Diego in which Arleen and Dick lived. As we sat on a bench talking, the thought suddenly came to me, as part of the Father's Christmas gift, *Here is a mirror for you to look in to see your perfection.* The mirror was Arleen. In some real sense, I knew then that Arleen had been given to me as a gift.

Late in January, Arleen came to Denver to meet Laurel, to see the retreat site, to explore job possibilities in the area, and to see if there was a way she could work with us in the center. While she was there, we had a number of meaningful experiences.

Christian and Jew

I had learned that Arleen was a Jew during my visit in San Diego over the holidays, and I shared with her my feeling that if indeed there was a work for us to do, being Jew and Christian was an important factor in it. I also felt Jim to be an integral part of that linking up of Jew and Christian, though I didn't know exactly how yet.

Jim had long been a great champion of the cause of Israel and a good friend of Jews in the United States. It was he who had introduced me to Judaism, and during our study of the historical Jesus, I had come to experience my oneness with Jews, and Jesus as the direct, conscious link between Christians and Jews.

Jim, Scott, and I had all felt that our book, *The Wilderness Revolt*, would make a contribution to the rediscovery of the common history that links Jews and Christians and reveals our unity. We looked forward to a time when the divisions between the two religions would dissolve into new appreciation of the role each plays in the spiritual evolution of mankind.

Now I sensed that the thread of my life and work with Jim was being picked up through and with Arleen. Perhaps she and I would play some role in bringing about this new kind of understanding.

One night Arleen was sharing some deep experiences of pain and trauma from her early childhood. I suggested she could give her Little Self, the child within, new birth, and be her own mother this time, raising herself in love as she wished she had been. She proceeded to do just that, and the result was a deep experience in which she felt born again as a new child within and to herself.

As she began to come out of her experience I said, "I'll tell you what. I'll be your godmother."

"What's a godmother?" she asked.

"A godmother sees that you get a religious education if for some reason your own parents cannot or do not. Since you had no religious upbringing, and I did, I could educate you in both Christianity *and* Judaism."

It was then that Arleen recalled, in a burst of exuberant delight, what a psychic friend of hers had told her more than six months before. Arleen had asked her friend if she knew who the woman was who kept showing up in her paintings. The friend had replied, "Yes. She's someone you have not met yet. You love her very much, and she loves you. She is your spiritual godmother, and you will work together."

We had a growing conviction that there was nothing accidental about our meeting, and that it was only a matter of time until the "Plan," the perfect pattern, would become clear to us.

Movement Toward a New Union

One other experience of importance happened before Arleen returned to San Diego. We had been sharing deeply about our openness with each other and to whatever work there was for us to do together. Suddenly we were enveloped in a circle of Light that penetrated both of our bodies and linked us together as one. It was as though the very molecules of our beings were being intermingled, uniting us as one person.

It was a kind of "marriage," but not a marriage like either of us had ever heard of before. It was a spiritual union of our inner beings, manifesting on the physical plane but not sexually.

We were in a state of ecstasy, joy, and peace when the Light "dimmed," and we stood in awe at what had happened. I had a strong sense of Jim's presence there, and I kept feeling prompted by him to give Arleen some token of our union. I asked in my inner being what I could give her, and the answer came immediately—the opal necklace I was wearing.

I had not taken that necklace off since the night of Jim's and my wedding. It had been his gift to me as his bride. *Not that*, my Little Self balked. *That's one of the few things I have that Jim selected for me and gave me himself.* I asked again and again what I could give Arleen. The answer that came was always the same.

As Arleen was packing to leave the next morning, I went into her room with the gift. I put the necklace on her and told her where it had come from. I also told her that I felt it to be as much Jim's gift to her as mine, since the feeling that it was he who wanted me to give it to her was so overwhelming.

Within a few days after Arleen left, the plans for our

center in Colorado began to disintegrate before our eyes, like sand slipping through open fingers. One thing after another came to light or fell away, making it more and more clear that the center would not come into being as we had thought. By February 15, I had decided to leave Colorado and return to the West Coast. The change, of course, was abrupt, but perfectly clear. It was as if my move to Denver had been only the first stop on my journey to a new life.

Dreams I had had during that time had been indicating a big change, so when it came I was not entirely unprepared. Since I did not know what lay ahead, I sold everything I had except my books, and took with me only what I could carry in my car. That was another big step toward freedom, and a further disengaging from the "things" Jim and I had shared, but this time the decision to let go was much easier.

As I started west, I pulled a trailer behind my car in which I had the files and office equipment that belonged to The Bishop Pike Foundation. Almost immediately, I began to have car trouble. I spent almost two entire days in filling stations, waiting for my car to be fixed. Finally I said to my Higher Self, *What's going on here? There must be some important message in this for me.*

The answer came immediately: *You are overburdened by the weight of the Foundation. You must get rid of it.*

At once my Little Self concurred: *If you'll just let me get to California, I will close the Foundation and let go of it all,* she offered.

Within the hour the car was ready to go, and the remainder of the trip was completed without incident.

9

BUILDING A NEW LIFE
A "Work" Emerges

JUST AS I WAS LEAVING DENVER, the advance copies of *The Wilderness Revolt* arrived. It was to be in bookstores by March of 1972, and Doubleday had set up a whole series of TV, radio, and newspaper interviews for me across the country to correspond with the publication of the book. Doubleday wanted to publicize the book, and so did Scott and I. After all, this was our gift to Jim. He had wanted his thesis to be known. Now we wanted that for him.

In spite of my earlier decision not to appear in public again, I agreed to the interviews and also to some lectures around the country as long as I was traveling. Those experiences were mixed blessings. On the one hand, I rejoiced in being able to offer people Jim's thesis on the historical Jesus. On the other hand, there I was, speaking on Jim's behalf again, being his spokesperson. I wanted to do it as a gift *to Jim* but not as a substitute *for* him.

One evening I was lecturing at a Jewish Community Center in St. Louis, Missouri. Before going into the auditorium, I was taking some time to "center in" in quiet and alone. Suddenly I was washed over by a sense of Jim's presence with me.

I welcomed him in joyful delight and love. *Say whatever you would like tonight,* I invited him, feeling I wanted to share the event with him.

I felt Jim close all during the talk, and I loved the sense of his being there. At the end of the talk, several people made a special point of telling me that they were old friends of Jim's, or had heard him speak many times, and that they had almost felt they were listening to *him* that night. One man said, "When I closed my eyes, I could have sworn it was Jim talking, so like his were your inflections and expressions, and when I watched you, I saw all of his most familiar gestures."

Jim had indeed been with me. That was not the only time, but he had been especially present that night. Whether his "presence" was only a matter of my holding him in my consciousness, or whether there was some sense in which "he" was there, is not really important. That I sensed him, and others did, too, is all that matters.

There was comfort and joy for me in that experience, and yet there was pain. For where was *I?* How was I, Diane, being expressed if even *I* saw and felt Jim in me?

Noncoincidental Coincidences

Scott, who had coauthored *The Wilderness Revolt* with me, had flown to New York with me for the beginning of that interview and lecture tour. He took part in several of the interviews with me and shared in that first week of excitement over the launching of our book. Then he had to return to the West Coast.

Arleen Lorrance had also accompanied us, but for another reason. She and I were still getting acquainted and leaving ourselves open to what our "work" together might be. Since Arleen had never experienced me as a lecturer and knew almost nothing of my life with Jim, I invited her to come along on the trip to the East as a way of getting on the inside of one whole dimension of my life rather quickly.

176

Late in February, after I returned to the West Coast from Denver, I had gone to San Diego to spend a few days with Arleen and Dick. The three of us had left there in two cars to spend a day at Disneyland before scattering in three different directions.

As we were preparing to leave the motel we had stayed in, Arleen was out, packing things in the trunk of my car. The door to the motel room stood open. I was standing in front of the mirror brushing my hair. Suddenly, with my inner ear I heard Jim say, *"This* [meaning the work Arleen and I would do] *is what you and I are doing together."*

I was overwhelmed. I had not even been thinking about Jim in that moment, and Arleen and I didn't even know what work we would be doing. I recalled the dreams I had had soon after Jim's death, in which he had told me that the work we had started to do, we would still do. I had not thought of that for a long time. Now suddenly here "he" was, confirming that that work was indeed coming into being.

I was debating whether or not to tell Arleen what Jim had "said," when Arleen stepped to the door. "What happened?" she asked.

"What do you mean?" I responded in surprise.

"Well, I was standing by the trunk arranging suitcases when something said to me, 'Go ask Diane what happened.' So I did," Arleen said matter-of-factly.

As we climbed into the car and started on our way, I spilled out the story to her. I was dropping Arleen off at the airport in Los Angeles on my way to Santa Barbara, and the entire trip was spent in a mad rush of excited conversation as we began for the first time to put pieces of "noncoincidental coincidences" together in a systematic way.

We realized that Arleen's spiritual awakening in the fall of 1969 had come in precisely the same week that Jim made his "breakthrough" to new life as his body died in the desert; that Arleen's decision to give up all anger, hostility, and violence and be totally open and vulnerable all the time had been made at the same time as my decision to "plunge deeper" in Israel; and that Arleen had received the gift of THE LOVE PROJECT as a way to be actively loving in the situation where she taught school, during the very same week as I had my insight about living and walking in the Light as *the* way for me. Then there were the paintings into which my face "painted itself" and Patricia's strong intuitive feeling that I had to meet Arleen, and all the events of our sharings which had followed.

We were almost overwhelmed with the sense of being part of a larger pattern. The picture puzzle of our meeting had begun to take shape.

Two by Two

Arleen had flown off to Redding, California, where she was scheduled to do a week of sharings in high schools and community groups, telling the story of THE LOVE PROJECT as it had manifested at Thomas Jefferson High School in Brooklyn. At the end of the week, I went to pick her up so that we could have more time for sharing and exploring together.

As we drove south down the northern coast of California, I told Arleen I wanted her to experience what we used to call as youth a "Redwood Cathedral." In the midst of a deep part of the forest, we parked the car and walked until we found a circle of redwood trees. Redwoods replenish themselves by sprouting circles of small trees around a large "mother" tree. Then if the mother tree is felled, or burns, what is left is a ring of tall trees, arching their leaves toward "heaven" like spires of a great cathedral.

We lay down on our backs in the moist pine needles and basked in the silence of the forest. The sun burst through above in a *Shekinah* of bright light falling in rays through the treetops above. Arleen said, in a hushed voice, "We are not alone here."

I, too, felt a presence. Was it Jim?

Soon Arleen began singing the Lord's Prayer. I joined my

voice with hers, and as we sang, I felt my heart to be wide open to the magnificent Life Force of the universe, to "God Himself." I thought, *When I pray like this, something almost always happens in response.*

The song-prayer ended, and suddenly "Jesus" stood beside me. I did not see him with my physical eyes, but I "saw" him, nevertheless, in that inner mode of seeing with the "third" eye. His shoulders were strong and muscular, giving evidence of a man who had done hard labor, his face was etched with lines of a deep compassion that could be born only of suffering, and around him was an air of gentle tenderness that spoke to me of the child in the manger.

As a child and youth I had longed for such an encounter with Jesus, but it had never happened. Now "he said" to me: *"This child* [indicating Arleen, who still lay on her back before me, absorbed in the silence] *has been given to you as a special gift. Treasure her."* Then I felt him to be saying to me: *"Now you are ready to go out two by two."* It was as though I had grown enough in my understanding to be entrusted now with his "mission"—to go out with another "disciple" to spread the good news that Love is in the land.

I shared the experience with Arleen, and another piece fit into our larger-picture puzzle. And so it had been decided that Arleen would join me on my trip to the East. We would see what more there was for us to see.

Links in the Past

While we were in New York, more pieces fell into place. I had told Arleen that there was a church I wanted to take her to which had been especially meaningful to Jim and thus to me. It was an Episcopal church where High Mass was still celebrated with bells and incense and processions, and Gregorian chants were still sung by the choir. Jim had loved the high ceremony, and I had come to love it, too. When we were in New York, we had gone there to services, as it was one of

179

the few places we knew to have that particular experience of "holy mystery."

Arleen had wanted to take me to a church, too. It was across the street from the School of Performing Arts, the high school from which she had graduated, and she had gone there as her refuge from the noise and rush of the city from the time she was in high school on. It was for her an outward representation of the inner holiness and spirituality she had only begun to discover in recent years.

The morning we were to go to "Arleen's" church, I awoke with a start, *knowing* that her church and Jim's were one and the same. "Where is your church located?" I asked Arleen. She told me. I didn't remember well enough where Jim's church was, and I hadn't looked up the address, but my inner sense was that they were the same.

We went by taxi to Broadway and Forty-sixth Street. As we walked toward Sixth Avenue, my knowing became even stronger. I asked Arleen a question I had asked before: "What kind of church is it?" Again she told me she didn't know. "Well, what do you want to bet that when we get there, the sign in front will say: 'Saint Mary the Virgin Episcopal Church'?" I said with growing excitement. Arleen just shrugged.

Soon we were there—standing before Arleen's church *and* Jim's. They were indeed one and the same. Again the puzzle pieces fell into place. Out of all the hundreds of churches in New York City, it was indeed no mere coincidence that the church that had been so meaningful to the three of us was one and the same. We felt the deep, underlying linking of three lives on planes "above" or "beyond" this conscious one. Somehow our lives had been intertwined long before we had met one another.

Again I was struck with the pervasiveness of the evidence—which I was becoming more and more aware of—that there *is* a pattern into which all my life events fall. Grief had really opened me to that sensitivity to the larger picture of things, the perfect pattern into which all experiences fit when I am willing to be open to them. Before Jim's death, I had tended to look for meaning in the events themselves as though they were isolated from the rest of my life. Now I was seeing over and over again that *everything* has its meaning only in the light of the overall pattern, and that my sensitivity to this depended almost solely on my willingness to look and see, to ask and receive.

Perhaps there is a special opportunity for us when a loved one dies, in that the event is so enormous in its import for our lives that we are almost forced to take a new look at things, even if that wouldn't ordinarily be our inclination. Many people begin raising the "big" questions by asking "why?" Why would he be taken now? or Why him? or Why us? And inevitably, the answers to these overriding questions must be found within ourselves.

I did not think of Jim's death as being of importance, in terms of any *meaning*, to *my* life until I was deep into my grief. I had sensed almost immediately that his death had been in harmony with the pattern of *his* life, but I never thought of the fact that it also fit into the pattern of *my* life in some overarching sense. Then gradually I began to see that his dying was not of importance to me *solely* because I was suffering as a result of it. There had to be some reason that we were brought together when I was twenty-eight, that we had had only three years together, and that now he was "gone." Moreover, it could be no accident that I had married a "famous" man and now had to deal with the consequences of that in my identity crisis and in trying to find my own way, my own work.

And now Arleen and I were uncovering what seemed to be a deeper pattern yet, which was the way Jim and I were related to and tied into *her* life even before we had met. Staying open to such "larger pictures" was one of the most profound aspects of my growth through grief and one of the enormous opportunities that await anyone who goes through such a major, life-shaking event.

An Objective Mirror

Arleen was able to be of great help to me as we traveled, for she could objectively reflect for me as I wrestled with my feelings of nonexistence whenever I was addressed as Jim's widow. She helped me to sort out my *feelings* from the facts of each situation. I began to get in touch with the ways I was contributing to my own sense of nonexistence by the responses I chose to make, or not make, in interviews. By not sharing anything of the "Diane" of me with persons who knew me only as Jim's widow, I denied them any opportunity to perceive me differently. I was very grateful for the Father's gift of this active mirror of my "perfection."

When I first began to be aware of my inner conflicts over being Jim's widow, my mind tried to build a case against my inner feelings by labeling me "selfish" and "self-centered." It would think things like, *You are just jealous. You want people to pay attention to you and not to Jim.*

In my Little Self I was afraid that this might in fact be the case, so I did not talk about my struggle, or even face it in full consciousness, until that struggle had been going on for over a year. But the motivation of egotism was too simple and obvious an explanation for what I was feeling. I had no negative feelings about Jim nor about being his wife; I *delighted* in him and in the love others had for him. I was glad people paid attention to him, for he was and is a fascinating and extraordinarily lovable person. And yet, I did not want to be known as his widow—or at least as *only* his widow.

I was not lacking in personal attention or affirmations of my own being. I was surrounded by love and by persons who cared about me and liked me for who I was. I had been all my life. Moreover, I had never really wanted to be a "public" figure. In fact, I felt very awkward about being set aside as someone "special" or "famous." I didn't feel "special" in the sense of being different from other people. I felt like the same "me" I had always been, just an ordinary person with gifts of my own to give, just as each person is uniquely important in the overall scheme of things.

This struggle against "widowhood" was really my own growth in self-awareness, self-understanding, and self-confidence. I was discovering who I was in new ways, and with an impetus that only Jim's death could have given me. It was for me to decide who I was and how I wanted to be me. I was being given the opportunity to *create my own reality consciously* as I built my new life without Jim. Surely this was a blessing, in spite of the pain it was causing me. This seeming *problem was indeed a great opportunity.*

Breaking Ties to the Past

I took another important step toward my inner freedom to be myself when I finally mustered the Little Self courage to close The Bishop Pike Foundation. Upon my return to the West Coast from Denver, I had announced the decision I had made on the road, to close the Foundation. But I had set a date that was about six months away. In the meanwhile, life moved on.

Upon our return from the eastern trip, Arleen's husband Dick suddenly announced that he wanted a divorce. There had been no previous talk of such a break, though their marriage had been dramatically altered by Arleen's spiritual awakening and the birth of THE LOVE PROJECT in her. Now as quickly as plans for our center in Colorado had dissolved before my eyes, Arleen's marriage disappeared before hers. In two weeks, the divorce had been filed and they had moved out of their San Diego apartment, putting their furnishings in storage.

Arleen then quit her job in order to be open to the new

that was emerging. It seemed clear to us that there was no accident in our both being left free at the same time to move in an entirely new direction. At first we thought perhaps The Bishop Pike Foundation could be the vehicle for our "work," so we began developing a plan for a new Foundation program centered on Love.

This was clearly not in harmony, however, with the Higher Self directive I had received earlier to close the Foundation, and nothing went well for us in that venture. When something is in harmony with the larger pattern, doors open easily; when it is not, they close in my face. My friends in Santa Barbara who were related to The Bishop Pike Foundation seemed to resent my having brought in a "stranger" who had had no association with Jim at all while he was alive, to work with me in developing a new thrust for the program of the Foundation. They made it quite evident that they were not enthusiastic about the new course I was taking.

For two and a half years I had chosen to allow the democratic process to determine the course of the Foundation, leaving final decisions to a vote of the Board of Directors, which was formed of persons loyal to Jim and his memory as well as caring for and loving of me. Each time they had decided to go on with the Foundation and its work, however, I had felt more and more put upon. I had wanted out from under the burden of the Foundation since the time of Jim's death, and it weighed heavier on me as time wore on.

Now I had moved ahead with a strong inner sense of direction, and the response of my friends was less than enthusiastic. One day in May a critical comment by one of my friends and co-workers served as the last straw for my Little Self. The balance shifted from her desire to please others and to let everyone have a say in the decision-making process, to a feeling, not that she *could* not go on, but that she *would* not.

I called an urgent meeting of the Board of Directors and announced my decision to them: the Foundation would be closed at once. It is no wonder they were surprised at my sudden change in approach. They experienced me as cutting them off, and indeed that is what I was doing. I did not even invite them to share their reactions to my decision, though they did that anyway! I had come to a new inner strength out of which I could make my own decisions, and I did.

On My Own Authority

I was greatly relieved to be free of the Foundation at last. I recognize now that gaining the inner strength to assert my own wishes and convictions was an important part of my recovery from grief. Jim and I had never intended to form something that would bind or limit us in any way. To the contrary. We had wanted a vehicle that would facilitate our ministry, our service.

I felt that Jim would have supported me in my decision to close the Foundation, for he and I had discussed it as a temporary instrument for our use and the use of those who wished to share our ministry to Church alumni. It was ironical, therefore, that I had felt I needed to assert my own will against those persons who wanted to keep the Foundation alive as a tribute to Jim.

This was just one of the many paradoxes of my grief. Over and over again I felt that Jim would have understood me perfectly. He would have encouraged me to do my own thing and not to be bound by any past, even my past with him. That was his whole approach to life.

But Jim was not there, and now all of us who had known and loved him were speaking for him: "This is what Jim would have wanted." Somehow that seemed absurd. It was like marshaling authority for what we really wanted to do ourselves. I wanted to avoid that kind of jousting. I wanted to stand on my own feet. Therefore, I waited until I had the strength within myself to say, "This is what *I* want," rather than, "This is what I think Jim would want." To come to that point had taken me two and a half years.

I have known other widows who have gone through similar struggles regarding their husband's business. Certainly in the dynamics of family relationships the same struggle comes into play when mothers tell their children, "This is what your father would have wanted," or the children say, "Dad would have let me do so and so." Mustering the strength to act on your own authority, without needing to convince others that this is what your spouse or parent would have wanted, can take a long time.

One of the things I became acutely aware of after Jim's death was how thoroughly each of us lives inside our own reality. Fifteen of us could be relating to the same man and have fifteen different understandings of him, fifteen different interpretations of his actions and motivations, and an incredible number of different feelings toward and about him. Remove the man from the scene, and we are left with only our own interpretations of him. That is shaky ground to stand on for decision making.

I had been acutely aware that I had only my experience of Jim to go on right from the start. Though I felt totally at one with him and thus felt I knew him as well as, if not better than, perhaps anyone else ever had, I knew him only as I knew him. Other people's experiences of him were equally valid for them. I therefore avoided using Jim as I knew him to bolster me up in any of the decisions I had to make for myself after he died.

That I had an active experience of Jim's presence in what was emerging as the work Arleen and I would do together seemed difficult to share without taking unfair advantage of the sense of love and loyalty people had of and to Jim. They had to come to their own peace with my new decisions, just as I had to come to mine. Thus I shared the inner experiences of the ways I had felt Jim to be a part of my coming together to work with Arleen with only two persons—Scott and Ellen Downing. To others, and to the Foundation members in general, I said only that I felt Jim's presence with me, and that these were my new plans.

Never in that effort to free myself from bonds to the past did I allow my Little Self to blame others for the struggle I was having. I knew in my Higher Self that the adjustment was mine to make. Yet my feelings were so often confusing to me, they must have been most disconcerting to friends and acquaintances who could not have known what was going on with me. To this day, people still ask me what happened to the Foundation and why we closed it. From where they were, many would have liked it to go on. I have had to use pure Higher Self strength to keep my Little Self from feeling guilty for not meeting other people's expectations and desires.

My family stood fast through all of this, giving their loving support to me no matter what I decided. My mother was especially eager that I not limit myself to an identity as Jim's widow. "You have your own life to live," she kept saying. "Jim would want you to make your own contribution." I was and am very grateful for this support, because I wanted to make my own contribution and appreciated my mother's affirmation of me in this, in her own name and even in Jim's.

I felt totally clear and at peace in my relationship with Jim. There were no conflicts there, no feelings of guilt. I felt I knew how he felt and would feel. I knew he would want me to get on with my own living. I sensed his participation in bringing this new phase into being. Yet it was because people identified me as Jim's widow that I felt it difficult to be who I was, and that paradox was what was most confusing of all.

A New LOVE PROJECT

One day in June, after the decision to close the Foundation had been made and while Arleen was in the process of writing the story of THE LOVE PROJECT* in Brooklyn in book form, I had an idea. "How would you feel," I said, "if we called our work together 'THE LOVE PROJECT'?"

* *The Love Project* by Arleen Lorrance, L.P. Publications, P.O. Box 7601, San Diego, Ca., 1972.

Arleen looked up from her writing, breathed deeply, and said quietly, "That feels right on."

We had no idea yet of what we would do, or the form it would take, but we were determined to put our minds to these questions as soon as Arleen's book was finished. Before the end of the month, we had laid out a plan for the services we would offer people as our manifestation of THE LOVE PROJECT. We had printed an announcement of our plans to be sent to all who had been members of The Bishop Pike Foundation and to all who had been on Arleen's mailing list to receive news of THE LOVE PROJECT. We were scattering the first seeds of our new work. Now we had only to wait for them to begin to flower.

We decided we needed a place that could serve as our "headquarters." Since we intended to make our services available to people all over the country, we knew we would be traveling a lot, and we wanted to be near a major airport so that travel would be easy. Arleen had moved to California from New York in order to have warmth and sunshine in her life, so we wanted to be in a mild climate. And I wanted to locate in an area where I could make a new start—that is, someplace where Jim and I had no roots together.

We had almost decided to settle in the San Francisco Bay area and had, in fact, made a down payment on an apartment. But before finalizing our plans, we took a trip to San Diego to see if that might be a possibility. On our way down the coast, I told Arleen, "I feel there is a house waiting for us there."

"I thought you didn't want to get a house," she replied.

"I don't, but I just have this strong feeling there is a house waiting for us."

And so we were guided to our "home base" in San Diego. The first day we looked for a place to live, we were taken to a house that was for sale. When we walked in the front door, I knew this was the house that was waiting for us. We continued our tour through the various rooms, and Arleen also began to sense it. By the time we had seen the gardens in the back, we were both saying, "We'll take it." We gave it the name Gentle Haven, for it would be our quiet place of retreat and rejuvenation between our travels.

A New Beginning

I had looked forward to San Diego as a place where I could begin again as the "new me," for I knew almost no one there. As soon as I began meeting people, however, it was the same story over again. "Are you *the* Mrs. Pike?" "You're not Bishop Pike's widow, are you?" "You're not by any chance related to Bishop Pike?" Or, "I'm so glad to meet you. I've long been a great admirer and follower of your husband." And, "Oh, Mrs. Pike. Your husband has had such a profound influence over my life."

Sometimes I would deliberately give only my first name when I met people. That would work well in the beginning— and sometimes for months. Then one day, the person would come up to me and say, "I just found out who you are. . . ." "Who I was" was the widow of Bishop Pike!

There was no way for me to escape dealing with my identity crisis. By then I was wrestling consciously and openly with my feelings. I did not like my feeling uncomfortable being Jim's widow and not knowing how to be who I was apart from that. But I did recognize my quandary for what it was: a real opportunity to come to a new sense of myself which would include my having been married to Jim and therefore being his widow.

Several people suggested I change my last name. I considered that, but the idea didn't feel right to me. In no way did I wish to disidentify myself from Jim, which was how giving up his name would feel. Moreover, I really felt that Diane Kennedy Pike was my name now. It felt good to me. It fitted. No, the answer lay inside me, not in the name itself.

I made big strides forward by separating my feelings from the intentions of others. I came to see that just because I awakened people's memories of Jim didn't mean they did not recognize me as a person in my own right. After all, they knew of Jim. They often knew nothing of me. Even if they first saw me only as Jim's widow, that did not mean they didn't soon experience me as Diane—if I gave them that chance. There was little difference between our discovering, as two strangers, that we had a common love for Jim and our learning that we shared a common home state, astrological sign, or occupation. Knowing Jim was a point of identification, a place to jump off from into the waters of new relationship.

Thus I began to be able to *receive other people as beautiful right where they were,* and to monitor my own feelings as *my* process, having little if anything to do with them.

Another Layer of Grief

I strained my back carrying heavy boxes of books while Arleen and I were moving into our new house in September. The severe pain that I suffered seemed to cause me to slip into a period of depression, pain, and low energy. After several days I realized that the day I had injured my back had been the third anniversary of Jim's death. It was as though my body were rehearsing once again the pain of that eternal week three years before. I was grieving again.

My mind tried to argue that I had finished grief long ago and it was ridiculous to grieve again when three years had already gone by, but Higher Self took over and gave Little Self and body permission to experience the intensity of this new phase just as it came, with no censoring.

One evening I asked Arleen to massage my legs to see if that would relieve some of the pain. I lay down on the bed, and she put her hand on my leg. I shrieked in excruciating pain.

"I hardly touched you," Arleen said in astonishment.

But I was already into an intense experience of recall. I was suddenly on the hills above the canyon in the Wilderness of Judea, experiencing consciously the excruciating physical pain of what my body had suffered while it carried me out of that canyon. It was a dimension of the experience which had theretofore remained unconscious, and I thanked God I had not felt it before. The physical trauma had been enormous. Now I was in touch with that.

Bringing the memory of the physical pain into my conscious awareness seemed to break the depression, and before long I began to emerge again from the grief and the pain. Healing had occurred on still another level, and once again I stood in wonder at the intricacy of nature's way of healing. Bit by bit, as I was able to handle it, layer after layer of pain surfaced to be healed. All I had to do was to be willing to experience the pain and the healing. The rest of the process was guided entirely by my Higher Self.

I was also fascinated by the phenomenon of "anniversaries." It was almost as if the physiological organism—or was it perhaps a more general attunement of the psyche?—registered the cyclic process of unfoldment, and as I passed through that first week of September again, at each year's interval, the death/grief experience was reawakened, though each time in a new way. I have since read of others who have had the same experience, and once again I am amazed at the intricate fabric of life.

The Decision to Die and to Live

As the year progressed, I worked constantly on freeing myself to be me. Arleen—my mirror—was a tremendous help, for she was in no way involved in my past and thus could be quite objective about what I was going through. Gradually I began to gain perspective on myself and to have a new freedom to be.

Arleen and I began facilitating weekend workshops,

which we called "practice sessions," in the fall of 1972, three years after Jim's death, meeting with small groups of persons who sought to be more loving in their lives and who wanted to see if THE LOVE PROJECT principles could help them on their way.

In one of our first sessions, I had an experience that served as a turning point in my identity crisis. Arleen was guiding us all in a relaxation experience. Part of the intention of the exercise was to enable us to make new choices in our lives, to *consciously create new realities*.

I went very deep into myself. Suddenly I was back in the desert again, standing above the canyon in the barrenness. I recalled that I had made the choice there to live, and that over and over again during grief, I had chosen to live. Even when the desire to be with Jim had been the strongest, I had chosen not to die but to live.

Now in the silence of my innermost being I realized that I still had that choice to make. I decided to choose death instead of life.

As I lay stretched out on my back in a room with about twenty other people, I began to withdraw my consciousness from my physical body until I experienced it as a small, equilateral cross of Light Energy at the center of my chest, near the heart.

I rested there for a time, experiencing myself as that cross of Light Energy in the "heart" of my body. Then I withdrew my consciousness even more, until it was but a pinpoint of Light. Suddenly I felt utterly mobile in my consciousness, able to see in all directions and to move at will.

I began exploring my body from the inside, moving through my veins and tissues at will. I was fascinated by my detachment from "my" physical organism.

I returned to the center of my body again and, from that single point of consciousness, began to expand outward into the universe at large. As my awareness expanded into timelessness, I did not lose contact with what was happening in the room. I could see my body, the room, the others in the room. I was also aware of the words Arleen was saying, without actually "hearing" with my physical senses. The experience was not like being out of my body, for I was also aware of the inside of my physical organism. My consciousness had expanded from a point within my body and thus still included it. Certainly this was the essence of the death experience when it happens in full awareness. There was no breach in my awareness on this plane, but it expanded far beyond it and was no longer limited by the physical senses and the physical body.

While I was in the far reaches of consciousness, I became aware that the others had finished their relaxation experience. Arleen had urged them to begin to interact with one another nonverbally. They moved around, and two persons approached me. One took my left hand in hers. I was aware she had done so, but I was not "in" that hand. I knew it was cold and lifeless. She gently put it down on the floor again.

Another person approached my head. I knew he was working with my energy, attempting to "bring me back." In my awareness, I knew he could do nothing to bring me back into my body if I did not choose to return. I felt totally detached and free, both from my body and from the influence of others. I knew that the choice of whether or not to return to life in my body was entirely my own, and I was not sure I wanted to return.

Time passed. Others showed concern. Some talked with Arleen, asking her if she didn't feel she should "do" something. Arleen trusted my inner process and let me be. In time the group began to gather for feedback about their own experiences. With the same detachment and sense of freedom, I decided to come back.

I began pulling my consciousness in from the far reaches. Soon I was again the small pinpoint of Light Energy at the core of my being-in-the-body. I began to expand my consciousness into the body again. I was able to form the equilateral cross of Light and then begin extending it outward into the arms and into the trunk of the body and the head, but the process was slow. My body was cold, almost clammy, and lifeless. Reviving it was taking time.

Then one of the women came and lay down beside me. She was close enough to be touching my whole right side. Almost instantly, my Life Energy, my consciousness, returned to the areas she was touching. With great effort, I gradually brought the matching vitality to my left side as well. Once I was fully in touch with me, I slowly sat up.

I felt entirely different. I had a new sense of myself as a free, conscious agent. I was indeed whole, and the "master" of my life in the body, for I had experienced my freedom to leave the body and to return to it at will. Now I "stayed" with a new sense of who I was.

In one way or another, I imagine everyone who has fully recovered from grief has made such a decision to live again. Not all of us come to it in the same way, of course, but to choose to live, not just not to die but to *live* our lives, is essential to full recovery. Grief provides us with an enormous opportunity to get in touch with the power of the Life Force within us, and with our freedom to determine the course of our future by choosing to take charge of our lives in the present—to live fully and consciously.

My Own Potential

In the weeks and months that followed that deep experience of death to my entrapment in the body and new birth into my own freedom to be me, I sorted out layer after layer of my conflicting feelings about being Jim's widow. I began to feel more and more whole again, more and more fully me.

I began to bring new facets of my personality into awareness and to manifest them consciously. I discovered new avenues of creative expression, and I had found a work that was an expression of me in the wholeness of my life process.

I feel that one of the greatest opportunities that grief affords us is to discover our individual wholeness in new and

194

more profound ways, to find the fullness of our own potential as persons in our own rights.

Before I met Jim, I had already come to a secure sense of self. I had shared my whole self with Jim. When he died, half of me died with him, and the half of me that survived was a mixture of me and Jim. Grief was my opportunity to become whole again in myself—to incorporate all that Jim had given me into my new sense of self and to discover what more there was of me yet to develop and express.

With Jim, I had experienced a full union of my feminine nature with a man, and through Jim, I had experienced the full expression of my masculine nature as well. Now I had the opportunity to experience and express the balance of the feminine and the masculine in my own being—to be wedded within myself to my own Higher Self, or Christ nature.

It was in this regard that I eventually came to a new definition of the word "widow" for my life. In one of our weekend LOVE PROJECT Practice Sessions, I began to address myself as widow. What poured out on paper was this:

Dear Widow:

You are alone. What made you whole is gone. He who made you what you were is no more. You are no more. You are but a reminder of what once was—a half of the whole, left as a memorial.

You are a burden to the community. One to be pitied, cared for, looked after. You are poor and homeless.

You have no place among us except as a symbol of the past. You are a reminder of death—and that death is no respecter of persons.

You dress in black. You walk alone through the dark streets. Your life is empty. It has no future—only a past. Your head and shoulders are bent over with the pain, the burden, the sorrow.

You are but half a person—long-lived but insignificant.

You are to be pitied indeed.

Sincerely,
Diane

195

Out of the depths of my unconscious, where an imprint had been made by the race psyche, emerged this archetypal view of a widow. Everything implicit and explicit in the archetype is the opposite of what I know to be true of me, so it is no wonder that whenever someone called me widow, I automatically rebelled and wanted to say *"No!"* What I had not been aware of was that I was responding to an archetype that I carried deep in my own subconscious—one that I could not transform until it had come into the light of my awareness. That had taken nearly six years, during the last three of which I had consciously sought to get in touch with what patterned response caused me to block my energies at the word "widow."

Since the archetype came to light, I have been able to consciously and joyfully challenge its form and content by creating for myself a new image of what it is for *me* to be a widow. Without too much stretch of the imagination, I could link "widow" to being "wedded to the One," and thus feel that to be a widow is to be free of limited, one-to-one relationships in order to live in universal love, wedded to no single one, and therefore free to be one with all and with the All.

The process of this unfolding into the total fullness and wholeness of my own being has been the most exciting and growth-producing aspect of my grief.

The LOVE PROJECT has become a new way of life for me, one that I can share with others. Its six basic principles for living in universal love express the core truths of all great religions in secular language. Those principles are:

> *Receive all people as beautiful exactly where they are.*
> *Perceive problems as opportunities.*
> *Be the change you want to see happen instead of trying to change everyone else.*
> *Provide others with the opportunity to give.*
> *Consciously create your own reality.*
> *Have no expectations but, rather, abundant expectancy.*

Arleen and I meet with people in all walks of life, and we practice, alongside them, being actively and creatively loving in our everyday lives. Surely this is the work Jim and I had hoped to do together, but in a form I could never have anticipated.

Jim is often present to me, and I know that the lines of communication are always open between us. As I live in that awareness, I leave myself open to ever-deepening and -broadening modes of communication and relatedness with all persons everywhere. Grief opened me up to that. It was a land of great learning.

10

THE LAND OF GRIEF
A Gift of Life Itself

I FOUND a fine road map for my journey through grief in Kreis and Pattie's book *Up from Grief,* and yet there was a great deal for me to learn as I traveled. I was learning how to live in life-giving awareness: in the light of heightened consciousness, "awake" to new dimensions of being while in the midst of a time often called "troublesome."

To be aware of myself and the inner dynamics of my being, to welcome every experience as a new opportunity for learning and growth, and to be grateful for all I experienced as a gift of Life Itself, made of grief the spiritual climax of my first thirty years of living, learning, growing, seeking. And the learnings that came out of that experience were to light my way into a whole new stage of my life journey.

Knowing myself enabled me to keep perspective on the experiences of grief rather than to be overwhelmed by them. By choosing to have Higher Self be in charge of my life, I was able to be self-affirming even in the midst of what Little Self experienced as great pain and suffering. And when Little Self was open to Higher Self perceptions and perspectives, she was able to experience joy in the midst of and alongside her own pain.

I saw as never before that the energies that are manifested as feelings are tremendously powerful. Without them, I could do nothing on this plane, for I would have no self-starter; but if I had allowed them to, they would have ruled or dominated my entire life-experience during the journey through grief, limiting it to emotions that overwhelmed reason, perspective, wisdom, and will. By allowing them to be released under the wise supervision of Higher Self, I freed myself of emotional traps that could have held me captive for years. I was grateful to have seen so clearly the importance of channeling the release of energies that I form into feelings so that they do not become emotions—that is, crystalized feelings—and thus begin to dominate me by their intensity.

Grief was a confirmation that the body reflects all experiences, no matter what level of self they are received in or created out of. By being in touch with and aware of my physical body, therefore, I was able to know more clearly my emotional, mental, and spiritual states as well. They were "visible" in my body as in a mirror.

Grief also confirmed again and again that the logical mind, when exercising judgment over my life experiences, can inhibit natural processes of healing and growth. However, when put at the service of Higher Self, the mind can be a faithful, efficient, and obedient servant.

Higher Self is an utterly reliable source of guidance and wisdom for the living of my life. Higher Self is compassionate, understanding, loving, objective, wise, and all-knowing in relation to myself. Higher Self is the key to integration, unity, wholeness, and oneness, within self and with the All, or God.

These perceptions have served me well as I have moved on in my life journey.

Grief Itself

There were learnings more specifically related to the land of grief through which I journeyed in my new awareness of self. They are of help to me as I share with others who are

199

traveling there, and they will be useful for return visits I will surely make in the future.

I needed to set my own pace for the journey. It might have seemed to someone looking on from the outside that I was walking in place, or even dragging my feet, for I was not ready to turn my attention to the future for many months. But from inside the experience, I was moving as quickly as I could, covering enormous segments of land with a rapidity that used all my energy. Only *I* could know how much time I needed to make each leg of the journey.

Almost from the first week, people began to ask me: What will you do now? Will you remain in Santa Barbara? Will you sell your house? Will you go on with Jim's work? Fortunately my Higher Self fielded such questions and gave answers like: I am grieving now. When I have finished that, I will know. Or, I will stay in Santa Barbara until there is a reason to move elsewhere. Or, There will be time to decide that. Or, simply, I don't know. But it took much supportive counseling by my Higher Self to keep Little Self from feeling pressure from these questions and to keep my mind from jumping in to say to Little Self, *You should know; you should have an answer; you should decide.*

Perhaps people ask such questions because they wonder what they would do under similar circumstances. Or perhaps they don't know what else to say. But it would have been more helpful to me if they had said nothing at all, rather than ask questions about a future that at the time looked very black and uncertain to me.

The friends who were the most helpful were those who held me physically (a hug hello and good-bye did wonders for me); let me talk about what I was feeling, listening intently and saying little if anything in response (I just needed to be heard); did not ask me questions about matters that required decisions regarding the future; assured me they were there for me to call on when and if I needed them; did those things they felt inclined to do as gifts to me instead of asking what they could do; included me in invitations to social occasions just as if I were not grieving, leaving it up to me to decide not to go if I didn't feel like it; let me be with and in my pain and did not try to "fix" things or "make me feel better"; responded lovingly with their presence (even if only on the telephone) when I reached out for help; shared with me their own memories of Jim, talking about him naturally as a loved one we joyously shared in common; made decisions for me while I was still in shock, making certain those decisions were not irreversible so that I could change them, or deal with them later, when I was feeling up to it; let me make my own decisions and trusted me to myself when I felt like making them; came to be with me when they knew I was suffering or in need, or at sentimentally important times—often not waiting to be asked to come. (My close friend Betsy Koester, for example, thought ahead and planned to be with me on the weekend of Jim's and my wedding anniversary, feeling that it might be a difficult time for me.)

I found I did not have emotional energy to invest in new friendships during those first months of grieving, and therefore old friends became even more important to me. I appreciated strangers and acquaintances who respected my need for privacy.

One well-meaning acquaintance who tried to be "helpful" put me fully in touch with the above. After I returned to Santa Barbara, she came over and/or called at least once a day. The first call was all right, but after that I felt her to be a burden. I did not know her well enough to relax in her presence and just *be* in my pain (even though she assured me that would be all right with her), and I did not have the energy to "meet" her and get better acquainted. I knew she meant to be helpful, but instead I felt depleted in her presence. I finally told her so and asked her to leave me alone. I was doubly grateful then for all those other acquaintances who made one contact, one offer of friendship and help, and then left the initiative up to me. It was family and old friends I needed and wanted to be with at that time. With them I felt comfortable and comforted.

I realize the stabilizing effect my house had on me during grief, and selling it and/or moving out of it during those vulnerable early periods of grieving might have delayed the recovery process. I did not recover my inner equilibrium enough to make major decisions for well over a year.

It was a help to me at every point to have "work" to do. Carrying out responsibilities insured that grieving was not the whole of my experience or the only dimension of my life during that first year after Jim's death. It also gave me a feeling of self-worth and importance and purpose which was very important in sustaining my ability to be self-affirming.

From the inside of grief, there was no way to know how long the journey through it would be. It was helpful that none of my family or close friends tried to rush me or urged me to set deadlines and goals. As I look back, I feel I finished grieving in a relatively short time-period—nine months. I know of others who have taken as long as four years to move through their grief. It is important to stay fully in the process and not rush it if backtracking is to be avoided later.

Opportunities Presented by Grief

Grief, I discovered, is in large part an energy adjustment for the body and the Little Self. As the physical being of my loved one, Jim, was removed from the dynamic interaction and sharing of energies which had characterized our relationship as two who loved each other deeply, I, left in my body, underwent an actual "physical withdrawal" period. I labeled that process extraordinarily painful, primarily because I did not want it to be true. By resisting the change, I caused myself added pain. If I would have entered into it fully as a *creative adjustment* in my physical being, I could have rejoiced in the *experience* of the energy shift. My physical body was being made whole again; having died to one form of wholeness, it was being born to another.

I discovered, in the experience of grief, that precisely *because* of that physical energy shift and adjustment, I had an opportunity to come to a new level of self-integration and wholeness. Having deeply shared energy and vitality with Jim, whose physical form was now dead, and having known one kind of unity with him, I had the opportunity to discover new levels of wholeness and unity within myself, physically as well as emotionally, mentally, and spiritually. I began to discover and learn about the "marriage within," that spiritual union of the male and female component parts of my being which gives birth to the "divine son" or the "Christ" within. What my Little Self was perceiving as painful was actually the struggle of my inner being to give birth to a new me.

My emotional suffering was brought on by my having merged with Jim both physically and emotionally. Because our lives were intertwined in that way, I suffered when his "roots" in me were torn out by his physical death. His death was rather like having radical surgery to enable me to die to one form of living in unity and to be born to another equally beautiful one: the marriage within.

Little Self's failure to see this larger picture caused her to suffer greatly—and my body, too. Little Self sought to hold on to what was, to *have* Jim still, and to *hold* him. She accepted my mind's definition of a relationship and what she had *had*, and thus experienced the loss of that, feeling herself to have been separated from Jim.

In fact, Little Self never "had" Jim, so she could not lose him. That was a reality she and my mind created together after his death. If Little Self had been totally integrated with Higher Self, she would have felt the ongoing oneness with Jim which Higher Self knew to be the reality. She would have responded to the reality that Higher Self perceived with feelings appropriate to what *is* rather than to what she wished could be. I know that now because I have been experiencing that process in other situations.

Because Little Self *felt* a loss, she created additional pain for herself by leaving herself open to the mind's reasons for the *why* of her deprivation. With each alternative the mind offered, Little Self suffered an "appropriate" emotion: guilt, rejection, unworth, etc. In *fact*, there was no "reason" for the loss, because in life fact there was no loss.

Another way in which my mind contributed to Little Self's suffering was by bringing back memories that had deeply emotional impacts on Little Self. All feelings associated with those memories were experienced by Little Self in great intensity, and I was grateful that they were filled with love and joy. The pain I experienced was due only to Little Self's desire to hold on to the past. The mind accommodated those desires and increased the pain of them by asking, *Why did it all have to end?*

Had there been memories of times with Jim that had themselves been painful, or had I had reason to regret any aspect of our time together, I am sure my emotional suffering would have been all the more painful and more complex. Surely it would have taken longer to work through. My own experience with death and grief, then, has given me even keener motivation to live each day, in each relationship, as I would like to remember having lived and related, so that there will never be cause for regrets.

I have given thanks many times that Jim and I chose consciously to stay "up to date" with our feelings and thoughts so that we never had unfinished business with each other—not before or after his death. It was a lovely way to live together, and a grace-filled way to have parted at death. It is the way I choose to live the whole of my life.

If I had allowed my mind to unleash its large store of old "shoulds" and "should nots" on Little Self, it could have increased her emotional suffering even more. I am certain this happens to others in grief, for they have shared the process with me. But my Higher Self had my mind well under its control, and those old judgmental patterns had been safely set aside. In response to Higher Self, my mind performed the great service of recording the *natural* "logic" of the grief process as it unfolded before me. This contributed to my ever-expanding awareness of the Life Process itself, and to my compassionate understanding of others as they go through grief.

I did not fear for, or worry about, or suffer on behalf of Jim after his death, for I knew in my Higher Self that life is ongoing. I did not suffer doubts and questions of a philosophical nature: What is life? What is death? What is the purpose of living? I did not lose the center of my own life, or my own sense of purpose and direction, because of the death of my loved one. I did not experience the meaninglessness, hopelessness, and sense of futility suffered by many who grieve. I never felt there was no reason to go on living.

These were the blessings Higher Self bestowed on me because I was open to them, but they were also the blessings of having freed myself from the mental limitations of former beliefs and concepts that would have added to my pain in grief. If I had still believed that "God rules the world," for example, as some "being" outside the Life Process of which I am a part, I might have tortured myself with the question: "Why did God take Jim?" Or: "Why would God do this to us?"

But I had reprogrammed my mind before Jim's death came so that it saw Jim and me as active, conscious agents in the creative process by which our lives were being brought into manifestation. That is, God was and is *within* us, and what *we* bring into manifestation is what God is doing in our world. We had made choices in harmony with the highest and best we knew and understood at each point along the way. All was a part of our learning; each opportunity for growth was to our advantage. There was no one to "blame." There was only the here and now moment to receive in gratitude as the ongoing process of our lives. I had a sense of continuity and direction, a confidence that everything was happening in accordance with some larger order and pattern.

Had I not already received the gift of these new knowings and understandings about the nature of life and death, however, grief would have provided me with a magnificent opportunity to expand my world view and to let restrictive beliefs and concepts fall away. For in the face of death, with a relationship with a loved one at stake, nearly everyone is challenged to reach beyond the boundaries represented by our physical bodies—the limitations of the five physical senses—to touch the one no longer alive and manifesting on this plane.

No wonder so many have written and spoken to me of their desire to communicate with the one who has made the transition of death. For the first time, often, they are turning their attention to that possibility, because for the first time, they feel the need or the desire.

If the full opportunity that these newly awakened desires to communicate in other than "physically" determined or limited ways is grasped and lived out in its potential, it can be the open door to a whole new birth into higher consciousness and the abundant life in the Higher Self, or God-Self, within. Such an opportunity knocks at the door of our awareness each time we struggle against "death" as that which puts an end to what we know as "life." Such an opportunity for spiritual unfoldment is one of the most challenging aspects of growth through grief.

Out of deep suffering, I learned deep compassion. Now I *know* from my own experience what depths of pain others go through, and I know how to be in understanding Oneness alongside another who grieves.

I spend my life, now, sharing with others the way I have found to *live* in joy, in the hope that all of us will have that

206

grace-filled experience of knowing that life conquers all forms of death when we choose life fully. When we make of our lives a LOVE PROJECT,* when we live in love, we *are* love and thus are one with God. There can be no higher consciousness than that, so let us give ourselves in love so that we might come to know fully that in all circumstances life *is* victorious!

* For further information about THE LOVE PROJECT, a way of life based on six simple principles of harmony and life affirmation, write to the author at P.O. Box 7601, San Diego, Ca. 92107.

MY GRIEF EXPERIENCE

General Characteristics:
Permeated with unpredictable feelings
Interspersed with irrational feelings
Not a time for major decision-making
A time of insecurity and low energy
A time of intense feeling

SHOCK		SUFFERING	
5½ weeks Sept. 2 to Oct. 10		10½ weeks Oct. 10 to Dec. 23	
Jim's Death	*Characterized by:* Numbness No Memory Recall of Jim Physical Re- covery Higher Self Joy "Pure" Grief	Onset of Severe Pain	*Characterized by:* Sense of Finality Intense Emo- tions, Mani- fested in Physical Pain Sexual Frus- tration Death Wishes Depression Low Energy Low Strength Low Resil- ience Rejection Feelings Guilt Feelings "Why" Ques- tions Aloneness Despair No Orienta- tion or Sense of Direction

	5 months Dec. 23 to May 30		June 1, 1970 to present
First Glimpse of Future Possibilities Without Jim	*Characterized by:* Building Strength Periodic Suf- fering Periodic Re- lief from Pain Missing Jim on More Romantic and Senti- mental Levels Emergence of Future- oriented Feelings and Thoughts	Begin Writing Book *TWR** and Building for Future	*Characterized by:* Future- Oriented Actions and Activities Major Deci- sions and Changes Intermittent, but Brief, Periods of Pain.

* *The Wilderness Revolt.*